Becoming
a Man Of
Power

Also by Matt Guest

The Face of Power

Becoming a Man of Power

Source

matt guest

HAMPTON ROADS
PUBLISHING COMPANY, INC.

Cover design by Marjoram Productions
"The Source" by Jeremy Dunn

Hampton Roads Publishing Company, Inc.
1125 Stoney Ridge Road
Charlottesville, VA 22902
434-296-2772
fax: 434-296-5096
e-mail: hrpc@hrpub.com
www.hrpub.com

If you are unable to order this book from your local
bookseller, you may order directly from the publisher.
Call 1-800-766-8009, toll-free.

Library of Congress Cataloging-in-Publication Data
Guest, Matt, 1964-
  Becoming a man of power / Matt Guest.
    p. cm.
  Summary: "An introduction and guide to the development and use of
personal power including developing spiritual energy and power from
all of our day-to-day choices including food, relationships, sex, and
more"--Provided by publisher.
  ISBN 1-57174-441-X (alk. paper)
  1. Success--Psychic aspects. 2. Parapsychology. I. Title.
  BF1045.S83G84 2005
  131--dc22
                                        2005019903

          10 9 8 7 6 5 4 3 2 1
      Printed on acid-free paper in the United States

Dedication

To Susan, Larry and Ann
for their never-ending support and eternal friendship:

I love you very much.

Acknowledgments

My deepest thanks to Matthew Genson and
Frank DeMarco for listening to the Source behind
the persistence, and for having the 'nads
and vision to publish this book.
Consciousness will never be the same.

Contents

What You Are Made Of • The Physical and Light Bodies • How
Free Do You Want to Be? • Fear • Expansion • Order • Community
• Manifesting • Your Life's Work • By Yourself

The Emotions • Frequencies • Listening • The Gift of Sadness
• The Earth • Chakras

What Is a Relationship? • Living Together • Dependence and
Attachment • Allowing • Doubt and Fear • Anger • Possession
• Dominance • Compromise • Coercion • Emotional Pain and
Sadness • Permanence

Sharing • Stubborn Lessons • Openness and Vulnerability • Arrogance
and Self-Esteem • Growing Up • Multiple Relationships, or When
One Partner Isn't Enough Drama for You • Motion or Stagnation
• Intimacy • Saying Thank You • Friends • Saying You're Sorry
• Love • Forever

The Illusion • The Riddle • Emotional Fear • Evil • Violence
• Reptiles

Preface

I'll be the first one to admit that this book is hard-core. This book is for men who want the most out of life, and who have a sneaking suspicion that something very serious is missing in their lives.

This work is not the final answer, and it is not intended to be. It is only what I have unearthed up to this point—a static snapshot within my own ever-evolving journey. So just assume that I'm talkin' smack, and use this work to rattle your complacent perceptual foundation to its core. Allow its alternative views to jolt you out of your own dogmatic structures and into a world of wonder, adventure, and awareness. And remember to retain your right to humor and enjoyment along the way.

Be sure to move slowly and deliberately through each section and procedure. Repetition is the key to reinforcing your new habits, just as it was in the creation of your old energy-wasting patterns. And be patient. Awareness is a process of evolution and ascension, and your life itself is that process.

Women can obviously benefit from this work as well, though it is not geared for them. But they will certainly find a lot of useful information and insights within.

Remember, it is *literally* all within you.

Introduction

The degree to which something is perceivable, palpable, knowable, present, obvious, real, or solid depends absolutely *on your sensitivity to its subtlety.*

This work is about seeing way beyond the veil of current and popular modes of perception into the hidden recesses where time stands still. It is about seeking out and touching the void—the intangible. If you're looking for the real adventure, this is a good place to start.

This is a practical guide. The methods themselves may seem elusive, but that is just the point. They *are* elusive—and unwittingly simple. Yet they are the most difficult tasks you will ever undertake. You will resist them to your core. You will resist order. You will resist silencing your mind. You will resist ceasing your need to rationalize and understand everything logically. You will resist solitude and lack of conversation. You will resist not asking why. Why? Because there are forces at work that prevent these things. They are unseen and innocuous—seemingly harmless or bland. They would prefer to remain that way for a good reason—to keep you locked in the darkness.

It would be immensely easier if these unseen forces were violent and obvious. Then they would incite you and arouse you to anger and action. But by remaining blasé and just outside your consciousness, they lessen your reaction and do not feed the flames of fury. In order to combat these forces successfully, you are required to muster your own strength and perceive the seriousness of the situation by becoming *more sensitive* through radical alterations of your current way of living and perceiving. You will learn to see things that others do not. You will learn to see them very, very clearly, and for what they *really* are.

This is an inner mystery. You cannot buy a product to take you there. You can't listen to mind-altering tapes or watch an instructional video. You can, however, take a formula that will assist you, but if you have not set your focus properly and you don't know where you're going, it will render you a recluse. You will become unhinged by your desire for silence in the midst of the confusion that is our world.

This *is* Power. This is the real deal. This is the ultimate journey spoken of by the ancients, mystics, and long-lost mystery schools. This is no joke and no half-assed weekend seminar. This requires undying commitment and complete immersion. It is elusive and difficult because it is so very, very hard to attain the required level of *inner* order. To any observer, you will appear to be wasting your time—doing absolutely nothing. But for you, it will become more exciting than *anything*.

You will permeate the sea of nothingness with everything you've got as you fish in the darkness. For a long time you will have no clue as to what you're reaching for. You are seeking an elusive frequency, a subtle vibration that has been reduced to a whisper within you and everyone else. But the procedures in this book will bring you close enough to it that you will have many opportunities to latch onto it and then feed it with your newly stored energy. Then it will start to grow. Mysterious and inexplicable things will start happening, new energies will suddenly appear in your life, and you will be able to create impossible situations out of the thin air. The possibility becomes the probability, and the probability becomes a chance occurrence. Eventually, it becomes the actuality, and then *your* reality and everyone else's fantasy. A mystery is nothing more than something forgotten.

This is so unbelievably subtle. It demands the nurturing of the utmost sensitivity in every aspect, from your emotions to your five senses and much more. If your life contains any distractions, you will miss it many times over. You will spend a lot of time alone studying yourself—every last nuance and the motivations behind each. By knowing yourself, you know the world.

Remarkably few have even glimpsed these possibilities. Our society's records contain accounts of mystics that happened across a faraway whisper. Most give it up and return to an easy life, surrounded by palpable comforts. Or they project their inner adventure outward onto the world and find some glamour and glory, but nothing of lasting value.

But if you persevere and *trust implicitly* your inner voice, you will be propelled into the most astonishing adventure of your life. This is no mental journey. It is the most intoxicating, multidimensional reality known to any consciousness in our realm.

Within you is the ultimate buried treasure, the pirate's keep, the holy grail, the philosopher's stone, the ring, the enlightenment, heaven, nirvana—the bliss. It has always been there. Once you uncover your first clue, you will be hooked, your energetic makeup permanently altered—you will never be able to return to the world of ordinary men and their insipid mindset. If you are ready to change everything you've ever known, if you are ready to nullify your past, if you are ready to finally attain your wildest dreams and live your ultimate fantasy, then let us begin.

Falling

The sky glows deep brown with faint crimson shadows. The freshly plowed and furrowed field extends across rolling hills in all directions, still damp from the recent rain. I watch without a single thought as the puffy auburn clouds move ominously in the light breeze that brushes the hair on my neck. The soil is rich, alive, and potent with the aromatic smell of minerals that I remember from my youth, back when the earth was filled with a deeper delight. My heart grows strong as I stand here, inhaling deeply, drinking in our mutual fondness.

A feeling from inside playfully invites me to fall backward onto the moist earth. I do, but nothing catches me, so I brace myself and land on my seat. There is disappointment in the air—I did not trust completely.

So I stand up, brush myself off, and try it again. This time I let go completely, trusting that I am among friends and forces greater than I. I fall thoroughly backward, eyes wide open as I watch the big chocolate clouds blowing over, lightning flashing within.

But just when I should have hit the ground, I pass right through, and find myself upside down and weightless in the Earth herself. I swim around, trying to orient myself, finally realizing that I am somehow floating and flying in a medium that is somewhere between water and sky—yet underground. I gladly glide and swim within this rich womb, frolicking and swirling, bathing in this luxuriousness, and I remember that it was only because I trusted.

1

The Basics

You have latent abilities and desires—a creative aggression within you. This creative aggression is beneath the subhuman aspirations and goals that you have inherited from a self-loathing society. You are so much more than you have *allowed* yourself to be. You are a shadow of your potential magnificence. The power within you is beyond your current level of awareness because you have blanketed yourself with a cloak of limitation in order to gain the acceptance and friendship of your peers and family—to get a job, get laid, and get paid. But you have forgotten who you are—you are a god.

The layers of reality are not layers of other worlds so much as layers of perception and ability. How is it that one person can see ghosts and another can't? It's not because one of them is crazy or has a magical gift, but rather because that person has been able to maintain a more subtle level of sensitivity along a specific vibration, and that vibration accesses what *appears* to be a deeper layer of reality. That vibration moves at a slower rate just under the radar of your brain because your brain is accelerated by thinking and electronic equipment. Because it falls under your radar, it *seems* invisible. Your internal organs and chakras must be relaxed, clean, and open enough to register and communicate energetic imprints. You are nurturing a broader state of awareness.

There are myriad possibilities awaiting anyone who desires to pursue them and dedicates their energy to the task. Things are only a mystery to those who have never pulled their head out of the sand. Your ability to perceive more fantastic Truths will grow as you live each of your previous ones. Don't shy away from challenges because they make you uncomfortable. Seize them, and consume their energy.

If you want to live in multiple dimensions—asleep and awake—then you have to cultivate sensitivity. Perfection is eventually required—this is a way of life, not an entertainment. At first—because you are fighting old patterns—it is *very* difficult and requires massive effort and concentration. You will be fighting against a creation that you gave life and energy to, and your creation is not particularly happy that you want to eradicate it.

But it does get easier over time. And then you will have to learn to stop fighting and struggling, and how to just let go and flow with things. Could you keep yourself from sabotaging it if it just fell into your lap while you were outside playing?

The most valuable real estate is inside you, and it can be touched. But it takes a monumental effort to shut the hell up and stop squirming long enough to catch a glimpse of it. There is no quick fix or drive-up window here. You've got to sit down, stop your internal chatter, focus, and never give up. If you do, you will start to see an entirely hidden world, one that's always been there but unavailable to those who have no inner discipline. You know it's there, so why can't you touch it? Why does it elude you?

You can't touch it because this world is inaccessible to people who have not faced their demons or their ruptured past. This is a built-in safety device—if you don't face your fears and walk past them, you will never have the Power. Occasionally, some maniac finds a few pieces of the Power and wreaks havoc somewhere. But even he has no idea of the magnitude of what's available. For every fear that you walk through and every bit of energy that you refuse to waste, a doorway opens, revealing a new mystery and a new piece of the Power.

Each person's path is a little bit different. If something in this book doesn't resonate just so with you, then play with it until it does—or throw it out. Don't force anything. Things always come back to you when you're ready. The important thing is to trust your light body and your feelings.

Enjoy your senses without being enslaved by them.

Eventually, as the gurus teach, you will be able to be solid around other people and let their personal crap pass right through you without being affected by it. In the earlier stages, however, it is very important to stay away from people that mess you up. The reality is that you need to be by yourself as much as possible while you thicken your new creation. Use that time alone to reaffirm, realign, reawaken, and stabilize your new energetic reality. Little by little, you will be able to be around others without losing touch with your new creation.

It takes time, persistence, and action to manifest things in the physical world. You cannot simply will something into being like you could before you got here. Often, people give up prematurely because others tell them "it will never happen, so get on with your life." But it's that kind of shitty mentality that keeps the human race from fulfilling itself. We already have everything we need, except for persistence and dedication to our vision. Don't *ever* give up! And don't ever let any half-assed jerk tell you to forget your dreams.

Let go of your need to have everything spelled out all nice 'n' neat for you. This path is messy and unpredictable. You have to learn to fly by the seat of your pants and grab things that appear out of nowhere. Your goal may not be a mystery, but the way that you get there sure as hell will be. Don't have *any* expectations about *anything*. Every time you think you've got it all mapped out, all you've really done is create a static structure within yourself. And your light body doesn't like that. Your light body will throw a monkey wrench at you just to tell you to *let go*.

And this is all a self-fulfilling prophecy is. You know you shouldn't try to make everything all straight and neat, but you do anyway—at some point in your life. And then it gets all screwed up.

You are not trying to be average—you're trying to be exceptional. So everything you do is exceptional. You make your body exceptional. You make your food exceptional. Your thoughts, goals, and dreams are all exceptional. The work you want to do is exceptional.

The hardest part for me was to let go of my desire to project my inward journey onto the world. Inwardly, I seek to create and live an adventure, utilize my sexual energy, and have power. Inwardly, these things are thoroughly fulfilling. If I project them onto the world, I can only approximate the fulfillment I can get inwardly. If I project outwardly, I find the glamorous Twinkie, but then crash from the sugar high and my electronically frazzled brain. The negative ego desires fame in front of others, regardless of the depth of its achievement. The light body and positive ego desire self-fulfillment and evolution—*depth*—with or without an audience.

My outward journey has now become secondary to my inward journey. My inward journey is my "real" life, and this is where I find my friends and family—whether they physically exist or not. I don't want to change anybody anymore. I just want to be the best that I can be.

Each section of this work can be used like a daily meditation. That's why the sections are short. Read one and carry it with you through your day as a key to unlocking something new. Don't force anything. Remember, your creation grows where your energy is focused. So focus on what you love and want, instead of on what you hate and want to eradicate.

As you create more and more space within, you will be tempted to fill it back up again. Space is unsettling—you are vulnerable and wide open. You have no chachkas to define yourself with, no crutches to prop yourself up with, and no reading material to distract your mind with. It's just you and the vastness. But it's time for you to enlarge yourself and allow your light body to fill up the space.

You search and search and search, looking all over until you find the treasure. Then you let everything else go—you sell everything you have. Nothing else matters anymore. You let everything else go so you can be alone with it.

Make the choice. Say, "This is what I want most in my life according to my heart." And then go get it. Beckon the transformation. Then strive to maintain the transformation. You don't let anything or anyone deter you. Nothing deters you.

What You Are Made Of

You are composed of a physical body and a light body. These realities are *not separate*. But for understanding of the nuances involved, the two terms are differentiated. Once their natures are understood, they must be remarried and allowed to work as a whole, and the terms can then be forgotten.

The Physical and Light Bodies

Your physical body and this physical world are manifestations of energy. Modern physics has already shown us this. Why does an atom have life force? What is the space that exists between a proton and an electron, or between two atoms, or between molecules, or between human beings, or between planets and universes? It is not space at all.

We have created this physical world as a stage with very defined parameters so as to play out certain lessons and repeatedly see the consequences of these self-created parameters. We have given ourselves limitation in order to *see past the limitation*. We have given ourselves fear in order to walk through it. We have given ourselves disease in order to rise above it. Complacency and our culture of mind-numbing, energy-sucking pleasantries have caused stagnation. In fact, we are absolutely boundless in our potential.

We have plunged ourselves into darkness in order to recognize the light, the power, and the potential. The evolution of your own energy and, therefore, the collective energy, is wholly dependent upon the choices that you make in every moment of every day. You must learn to see beyond this dream *while you are still in it.*

Your light body has its own destiny and its own agenda, and will act with unbridled creative force if you allow it to. Your light body is so much more than lucid dreaming, astral projection, remote viewing, or out-of-body experiences. It is your ultimate, complete, and strongest reality.

Knowledge is never outside you—you don't need to read books. You can learn in your dreams. Your conscious dreams will tell you everything you desire to know, even very complex things and things that have been long forgotten. Your light body is trying to remind you of what you already know.

How Free Do You Want to Be?

I want to be free from constraint, noise, anger, fear, and censorship from within and without. I want to be free from thoughts, beliefs, and expectations. I want to be free to roam, to dream, to love, to vanish and return at will. I want to be free to be quiet and to move as slowly and reflectively as I need to, to be contemplative and to stare into space without interruption. I want to be free to manifest my uncompromising vision, to practice the perfection of every little thing—every last thing.

Fear

Talking about fear with your therapist is not, nor will it ever be, the same as sitting by yourself in a dark room surrounded by your fear. There is only one way past your fear, and that is *by yourself.* Once you can sit in silence with who you are, and not feel the need to call someone, then you have walked through fear. Then nothing will ever faze you again. It is a truly worthwhile endeavor, and necessary for one who desires real power.

We like to hide our imperfections, to keep them pushed down to an unconscious level because we want to see ourselves as perfect in the eyes of others and their expectations of us. This is resistance to the fact of who we are—to the reality. Once you allow your imperfections to be known to yourself and others, then you have accepted who you are at this very moment. Now that you have allowed yourself to be imperfect, your awareness has instantaneously increased, and you are capable of *consciously* changing.

Expansion

Relaxation is a state of openness. It is a state of nonresistance. Relaxation does not necessarily imply nonmovement. The body can move perfectly at any speed if you work with it and do not resist its natural flow.

Increased energy heightens the receptivity of your senses, does it not? If you are relaxed and rested, food tastes better, sunlight feels better, the air smells fresher, your favorite music sounds even better, love runs deeper, and you're more at ease. You enjoy the little things more. You enjoy everything more. Passivity is a state of reception.

Increased energy heightens sensitivity. Increased energy heightens your reception to outside energy. But to store energy, you have to clear out some space. This means you have to let go of some things, like you do when you collect too much crap and you decide to have a yard sale before you move. It's time to clear out some of the useless knowledge, belief systems, good and bad memories, fears, patterns of behavior, compulsions, mental images, thoughts about Bob or Matilda, fantasies, and so on.

Now you have a little extra space inside and you feel somewhat unstable when you are all alone. Do you feel the discomfort that makes you want to reach for the phone? Do you feel like you might miss something important when you pull back from the television remote? Does the uneasy silence make you want to sit in front of your computer? Just sit down and watch what happens. Look at how you're holding your breath, how your heartbeat is a little faster and your muscles a little more rigid. Your mind darts around the room looking for an important distraction, something really major that can't be ignored.

Stop everything. Relax your body into the chair. Breathe deeply and let go for a minute. Look around the room and disconnect yourself from your mind's desire to latch onto something. Just observe. Now the room becomes a little more real. Sounds and smells move into your space. The colors are a little deeper. You feel a bit more at peace. Your light body has fused just a little bit more with your physical body because you have given it some space.

As you continue making space over the days and months—and not filling that space up with other stuff—you will feel "tighter" inside, more powerful and dense. At times, you will feel like you're going to explode. But don't release that energy through sex or work or thinking or indulging in fear or anything else. You have been living in a state of depletion for so long that an energetic state is uncomfortable and unfamiliar. Hold your energy, and then relax into it. Expand. Stretch. Break the boundaries. Become larger than life.

After a while, you may wonder if something is wrong because the expansion doesn't feel like anything anymore; it used to be so noticeable. But after the stretching is done (or between stretches), it won't feel like anything's going on.

Escaping from the physical form by focusing only on the spiritual is not the way to attain Enlightenment. Our challenge, rather, is to fuse the two in order to maximize our full potential.

Order

Establish order. Make a list of all the things you want to accomplish during your week. Allow your body to tell you what days are good for each item. Decide what time you should eat, exercise, balance your poles, recapitulate, clean your body, study, go to bed, and so forth. Plan your life and day on feeling-time, not linear time. Then set up your schedule.

If the schedule you create doesn't work, or if it stresses

you out, modify it until it does work. This is not about *forcing*. It's about *desire*. If you desire to advance, then set it up. Your desire will be your catalyst. Give yourself some free time to fart around. Don't be so strict that you get frustrated and throw the entire thing away. Be disciplined, yes, but not restrictive. Focus and *doing* are the desired results.

Community

Imagine what a golden age we could have right now if multitudes of people with inner wisdom and knowledge came together in groups and used their knowledge to work in harmony. Instead, each one wants to patent their creations and make a million dollars, competing with their fellow man. But you don't need a million dollars. All you need is wide-open space, food, and a safe, quiet home. Isn't that what people buy with their million dollars—space and a home? They want a place where they can be alone with their feelings, a place where they can relax and not be bothered.

You need space to commune individually with the Source. Then, when you feel whole, you will want to be with your family and friends. But if you compete with others, you create division, friction, unrest, resentment, and failure. In a competitive market somebody has to lose. This is why as a people we are failing. We have forgotten how to connect with the Source individually and then how to unite with each other. We have forgotten how to take care of the self *first*. If you are not whole, then you are worthless with others.

Manifesting

As far as the physical world is concerned, nothing is going to happen magically to elevate your state if you just sit around and wait for it. You have to go out and make it happen. As far as the spiritual world is concerned, however, you must allow it to manifest by getting out of the way. Spontaneity is allowing the light body to act through your physical body without prejudgment.

If you think it's okay to allow yourself to entertain certain thoughts because they're only thoughts, you will discover soon enough that they have become your reality.

Your Life's Work

There's nothing meaningful at all about drudgery, other than to show you that you believe drudgery is necessary if you want money. Why would you support a system based on fear and manipulation?

Defeated people love to say, "That's just the way it is. Just play the game." But you know what? That's *not* the way it is—it's the way we've *made it*. The way it *is* is the way of the Source, and I can tell you it is nothing like the way people have made it.

So if you want something else—something more—then you have to make it yourself. Everybody else is too whipped by the system. Why do people take vacations? Because their *real* life sucks! Why aren't you your own boss yet?

Jobs encourage or manipulate you into suppressing and repressing your chakra-emotions in order to be nice, civil, polite, or politically correct, and you are motivated to do this for money. Forget the money!

Our sterile corporate environs have robbed us of our emotional nature—not our indulgence in the five senses and pleasure but our vast range of chakra-based feelings and their ability to lead us spontaneously and naturally into unique adventures and playful exploration. We have been robbed of our time. And all these electronic office machines have interfered with our subtle abilities to detect nuances and energetic shifts.

Jobs are called *jobs* because they suck monkey ass. And it will *never* matter whether you are a corporate fast-paced multitasking piece of crap on a stick or a starving nappy-assed clerk at a hippie health food store—all *jobs* can kiss my hairy culo. You want to do something meaningful? Then find out what moves you and create your own reality and way of life.

Then you will be supported by those who wish they would've done it first, *and* you will have loads of self-esteem, confidence, knowledge, and something worth saying to others. That's right—create something out of the thin air and make it stick!

The means *is* the end! What you do is what you *are*. If you do work that you hate, just for money, then you are a whore. Working at something that is in direct opposition to your heart and light body is an aberration and will wreck your physical body. Trading serenity for a higher salary and a longer vacation means that you are living according to your fear. Working two jobs to make ends meet will frustrate you to the point that you spend even *more* money and dig a deeper pit for yourself. You'll eat out more because you have no time to prepare your own quality food. Then you will need those medical and vision benefits! This mentality is crap.

Getting *used* to something involves the cultivation of *insensitivity*—you are looking to gloss over something that irritates you. Why would you do that? Why would you want to train yourself to be insensitive? Cultivating the light body and intuition involves extreme *sensitivity*.

You increase your *strength,* not your tolerance or insensitivity! Increasing your strength is increasing your energy, and this raises you up. It does not dull you and repress your frustration. It does involve lots of hard work and a desire to rise above.

The challenge is in rising above and not running away anymore, to make it all work, to be superior *and* unaffected. It's not about letting negativity flow through you, pretending to be detached or some crap. It's about raising yourself up enough that you realize that negativity is nothing to get so upset over. In the grand scheme of things, it is insignificant—its energy is paltry. And yet, at this moment, it may be your greatest challenge.

You have to create your own world and your own rules. It will take some time, because you have to create your own network of people with the same interests so that you can manifest a living mass of power. But if you begin now—even if you do only a little bit—it *will* grow because there is passion behind it.

If it takes a while to find others who feel as you do, it's only because you haven't raised yourself up high enough yet. If you *do* what you feel, then others will be drawn to it. If you only *talk* about what you feel, so will others. You have to stick your own neck out and get busy.

Take care of what is immediate while also investing in the long term. The means will come when you do what you feel without fear of consequence. You are provided for.

By Yourself

Aloneness and silence will become places you look for constantly—nectars you long to imbibe. All human contact weakens you at this point, not because humans are bad, but because you are not yet *solid* enough in your new energetic configuration. You can still have contact, but if you feel yourself weakening or your energy shifting back into old or unnatural patterns, then you need to disconnect and withdraw until you feel solid again.

Stay clear of pornography and similar arousal during your transition. All your newly stored energy can easily wind up back in your sexual chakra with a vengeance. Eventually, this energy won't derail you. It's just a matter of balance as you redirect your energy toward its higher flow against the barrage of distorted energy that comes at you from almost every other human being. They are distorted, you are not, and you don't want to be. That is all.

Newborn

Note: *This dream occurred shortly after college and just before I began my quest for the Source. I have included it here because it shows so clearly how the light body communicates your present state via dreams. This was an extremely vivid dream.*

I am somewhere amidst the towering skyscrapers in downtown Los Angeles. It appears to be just before noon, but it's hard to tell. There is light on the buildings and sidewalks, but the tops of the skyscrapers are all dark. There are no clouds. There is no sky.

Everything seems bland: The air is not too hot or too cold; the skyscrapers are all painted off-white or light beige; there are no posters or billboards, nor are there any signs, cars, buses, bikes, or building numbers. Everything is coated in a fine sand or a heavy dust, and there are no people anywhere. Actually, there is no sign of life or feeling of any kind. The life has dried up. It has become a ghost town.

The streets that I'm walking down seem somewhat familiar. The buildings are concrete. Some have glass fronts. And there are papers everywhere—blank white and off-white sheets of office paper. They are all along the gutters and up against the corners of the buildings, like there was a tremendous desert windstorm five, maybe ten, years ago. Strangely, there are no shadows. But there is a light breeze—faint and barely perceptible. It carries a slight feeling of depression or foreboding, but not really.

Otherwise, it is deathly silent. I feel thoroughly barren and plain.

I stop in front of one of the buildings on the left side of the street. I look up its sheer side—its height is dizzying. I put my palm out flat on the wall and sense something alive, perhaps up at the top, or maybe a few stories down—but it's just a feeling. I really can't be sure.

And then, I hear something. It sounds like a cry, but it's so faint. I look around at the building that I'm standing in front of. It has a plate glass entryway. I walk over a few steps—the cry seems to be coming from inside. I pull open the heavy glass door and walk in. The light dust stirs a bit. There are papers in here, too. It doesn't feel that bad; the sunlight is lightly streaming in.

But now I can hear it. It sounds like an infant crying. It's so weak, like it's been crying for a very long time. But there are only papers in here. I use my toe and gently shift the papers and dust around. Nothing. But what's this?

I squat down and look. There is a piece of paper that seems to be twice as thick as the rest, like two sheets stuck together. I reach out and pick it up, blowing off the past. There's a little bump halfway down the page, about the size of my fingernail. The hoarse weeping is coming out of it. And then it moves! Ever so slightly, it shifts. And now I see it—it is a newborn baby, perhaps even just a fetus. But it is alive.

I stand up, holding the paper gently, stretched between my hands. I turn us both toward the sunlight to get a better look, and the infant squirms—no, stretches as the rays bathe its exhausted body. I walk out the door into the now caressing breeze. I put my finger on the infant, and it sighs in relief. I have touched a long-forgotten part of myself, and it drifts off into slumber as I put it inside my shirt against my breast and walk off with purpose down the shady, cool street.

2

Emotions and Chakras

I don't know where it is; I just know that it is. And so I reach out with my heart and find my way. And I succeed.

The Emotions

We have lost our range of emotion. It is buried and forgotten in this world of hurry up and wait. Get a job, buy a few trinkets, retire when you've got one foot in the grave, take a few trips with other convalescents on medication, and then suffer a long, nauseating illness before dying ignobly in an antiseptic room while people weep bitterly for themselves and wonder how much inheritance they will get. Is this how a man dies, like a putrid corpse totally robbed of all power and self-respect, a victim at the mercy of bumbling and incompetent people whose perception of health is a pill that gives you diarrhea and nausea, and ruins your liver and kidneys? Where's our birthright? Where's our magnificence?

When the words and the pictures have faded, what lingers inside is the feeling—the joy, the affection, or the loss. Emotions, properly utilized, lead one to Truth through the activation and cultivation of chakra energy. Each of your chakras is an emotional entity, with a richness and an identity. A lack of feeling indicates chakra shutdown. Repression is chakra shut-down. Depression is extended repression.

There are feelings, moods, and colors that you haven't felt for years. Occasionally, a blast from the past reawakens or reopens a doorway to feelings lost since childhood. An old feeling gets triggered and you wonder where it had gone. Feel these feelings to your bones. Live in them and encourage them.

Physical life is supposed to be filled with action and flow. But when there is little action and little flow, we substitute drama instead.

Emotions are not drama, but a full-bodied expression of life. It's like we only have so many modes of feeling any-more—we've forgotten the rest. But they're still in there some-where. We've just chosen to work with a handful of "safer" ones. We've lost the scope of what we are capable of. We're supposed to be treasure troves filled with colors and flavors. How barren we have become, how parched and flavorless! We need a revolution of feeling. Let's bring color back into our world.

Typically, we focus on feeling *pleasure* through our five senses. We believe that this is happiness. But it isn't. You need to go beyond your senses into a currently less tangible world of bliss. In this realm, each feeling has a unique sound or vibra-tion, a frequency of peace and fullness. When the chakras and their feelings vibrate together, they produce subaudible over-tones or harmonics that resonate outward, triggering similar vibrations in others. Now you know why some people are pleasant to be around, and others aren't.

The Source, if *allowed*, plays your chakras like a harp. If you are in a space with others who allow the Source to do the same with them, a living, breathing symphony is created. Back in the time of the ancients, people got the attention of the gods if their emotion was strong enough. The emotion carried a fre-quency, and different gods were partial to different frequencies and would tune into the person emitting the frequency.

But the more evolved "gods" have moved on. What we're

left with now are the less evolved ones, those energies that would seek to create dissonance within us and our communities. These energies play upon our five senses and dependence on pleasure, agitating our chakras—especially our mind-chakra—and causing us to produce frequencies that incite more fear, anger, hatred, jealousy, and drama. The frequencies coming from our electronic equipment are part of this dissonance. Negativity is a vibration!

Disruptive frequencies can also assist in pushing your light body out of your physical body. Now you've created hysteria in yourself and in others. Get away from the electronic equipment and get back in your body, because nobody but you understands at this moment how disruptive these things really are. These disruptive things have been camouflaged on purpose.

The range of chakra-feeling is what physically moves the mountain or levitates the stones—not willing it or thinking it with your mind. "Be the mountain" means to resonate at the same frequency as the mountain. When you are one with it, then you are in it and it will follow your will.

Do you remember your flying, vivid, or conscious dreams? Do you remember how much feeling was involved—how deep your emotions were? Feeling and emotion are the keys to the light body. Trust them.

Your feeling about something is the energy that you are projecting. Are you bitter about low income? More low income in store! Are you feeling like you have plenty and are free to do as you will? More is on the way.

Our feelings have been slowly diminished over time until now we are practically automatons with nothing but a few brittle and volatile emotional stragglers left to give us the impression that we're still alive. These relics rely on short impotent bursts of pent-up toxic emotional residue to trigger them. This is our narrow little world, our infinitesimal window of emotion.

All you need to do is look around at what is coming from others. Why do people play their music so loudly? Because all day long they've been told how to think and how to repress, and when it's their time, the last thing they want is to feel someone else's mood. So they select music that most closely approximates what feelings they have left, and they blast it in their cars and homes and push their mood outward onto others so loudly and thoroughly that no one can push it back.

And who plays their music the loudest? Teenagers and college students—the ones who feel the greatest insult as society seeks to thwart and stifle their essence at their most lively period of self-development, when they should be discovering who they are and what their light bodies want to manifest.

The greatest thing you can ever do for yourself is to allow yourself to live according to your desires—your *deepest* emotions. Do whatever you want within your world, and never think about the consequences. Never ask, "What if?" Don't ever mull it over. Just feel the pull and follow it, without reason, without rationality. It's fun, and always will be. You are not here to harm anyone. Your deepest emotions are *always* creative. They are never destructive.

If you lack energy, your pure emotional state becomes splintered. Then you get caught up in the ride of opposites: happiness and sadness, love and hate, anger and passion, euphoria and depression, drama and jealousy, or spontaneity and apathy. When you feel the onset of a negative emotion, take one step back and disengage. Become the observer, not just of yourself or the other person, but of the entire situation. See the hidden motivations, the secret agendas of all involved. By doing this, you will conserve energy that will enable you to transcend the ride of opposites.

When your energy is low, the pure round tones of whole emotions become brittle and fragmented. Then they have a tendency to cause negative reactions, inside and out. Full feeling-tones are cushioned within affection for life and development, instead of judgment and destruction. Encouraging and feeding full tones blows you out of your comfort zone and further into the adventure.

If you refuse to identify with any one *segregated* emotion at the expense of the others, then you have refused to allow your energy to be fragmented. This has nothing whatsoever to do with repressing emotions. The emotion is still real, present and active. You are simply choosing not to drown in it or be ruled by something impure. You desire to know why this trivial or petty situation has you by the balls, and how you lost sight of the bigger picture. You want to see something beyond the fragment. You seek to reclaim your wholeness and find out why your energy became splintered in the first place.

Let's say, as one example, that you had a crappy day at work and you drained your energy by squashing your own deepest feelings. In the process of doing this, you lost sight of your greater goal and desire—the big picture—and plunged yourself into a dark funk. You are now bitter and fragmented—splintered. You have created division within yourself and are no longer one with your lifelong desire to attain your *ultimate* destiny. You are no longer whole.

You come home and start to unwind, allowing the frustration within to surface, and you gradually become aware of how your physical body suffered because of this. You have gas, indigestion, hemorrhoids, bad breath, and your rash is worse than ever. You begin to see just how pissed off you really are.

Now your girlfriend comes home from work and she's cranky, too. She starts venting her anger, talking loudly, and throwing her belongings all over the space you just cleared for yourself. You can feel your breath shortening and your muscles tightening, and your anger is about to flare.

But then something truly magical occurs. Just before you lose control and explode, you make a conscious choice to seize the silence that exists *between* your escalating anger and any outward action. You choose to *observe* your inner frustration, and then you see hers as well. And you *feel* in your heart and other chakras that anger is only your reaction to your own inner frustration. It is a fragment that you have helped to create by denying yourself your complete emotional reality during the day. You are not mad at her—you are mad at yourself! So now you choose to keep your anger where it belongs—directed only at yourself. You choose to keep it there so that it will remind you not to do the same stupid thing day after day.

For her, you feel love and a desire to be at peace. You want to commune with the Source within her and allow your entire range of emotion to flow again. You have already walked through many fights with her, and they served no purpose other than to separate the two of you, further injuring your body with anger, stress, bad digestion, and troubled sleep. That old road was an immature way of creating a detached space where you could lick your wounds and heal from the crappy day that *you created*. You do not want to expend any more energy in creating and *maintaining* additional drama and conflict. You want to heal and move forward with your journey, completely undistracted.

So now you look into her eyes with affection, and tell her that you just need a little down time to unwind, reflect, and put your stupid, neglected self back together. You ask her, with affection and respect, please not to interfere with the space you have created by unleashing her own frustrations where you will come into contact with them—you ask her to respect your space and create her own. Now you have become a mirror for her, and she sees where her responsibilities are as well. You both want something more than petty dramas, and so each day becomes another opportunity to increase awareness, conserve ever more energy, and move closer to a higher state of being.

The object here is to make the most of this situation and gather the energy to become whole and tranquil. Quell the emotional *spikes*—positive *and* negative. Tranquility—inner peace and calm—is the state attained by one that settles beneath the choppy surface waves of fragmented emotions to a deeper, more subtle state of gentle stillness and breadth. In this state, you will become aware of more important aspects of life than superficial drama. In this state as the observer, you learn to listen instead of *react*. In this state as a watcher, you learn to hear the whispers of other energies, including the Source. From this state, you start to see the dream unravel. As a unified being with a single purpose, you start to lift off from your moorings to this physical dream.

Frequencies

We naturally produce, receive, and have the capability of interpreting extra-low frequencies, which are frequencies just below our audible range. It just so happens that nature is in harmony with this, producing the same inaudible and calming frequencies in the wind and water, along with the subsonic sounds emitted by whales, dolphins, ghosts, carrier pigeons, seals, and elephants. The king's chamber of the Great Pyramid resonates in this range, along with the vibrations of the inner Earth herself. Energy healers and other grounded people emit an abundance of these frequencies. One of the best conductors of extra-low frequencies is stone. Stonehenge and similar stone structures amplify the extra-low frequencies of the Earth.

Our current society and its focus on devices that scramble and elevate brain frequencies is in direct opposition to the natural healing and dreaming states that we are programmed for. Computers, televisions, cell phones, digital equipment, high-voltage power lines, fluorescent lights, microwaves, rational thought, excessive talking, the cult of hurrying, frenetic music and videos, oversexed advertising, and fast food are just some of the things that wreak so much havoc on what should be our natural low-frequency state.

If you are vibrating in the extra-low-frequency range, you are meditating. Staring is absorption, the process of *drinking* in energy. Meditation is vibrating at extra-low frequencies. The lower you go, the more you can communicate with the animals and the Earth.

Extra-low frequencies can be utilized and controlled *if you become them*. When your body hums in the low-frequency range, you become connected to the Earth and its creatures.

The higher frequencies are the frequencies of destruction, fear, and mind control. Stress, bacteria, and parasites resonate at higher frequencies.

You will find as you begin to resonate more steadily in the low-frequency ranges that, while many people like to hang out with you and enjoy the feeling of your energy, some people will try to disrupt your vibe or agitate your frequencies. These people will try to engage you with incessant or hyper chatter, or by trying various ways to get your attention. It's not that they're necessarily trying to ruin your groove, it's more that they don't know any other way to relate to you or to the depth of what they're feeling. Maybe you can show them how to chill out.

Listening

When you listen, there is no interpretation or evaluation of the words. There is only a *feeling* without conclusion or judgment. This feeling is what changes you, for the words themselves can never change you. Words are linear and have no force in and of themselves as angles or curves on a page, but the feeling behind them is energy and love, and will directly flow into you and tell you a story that you will not soon forget.

The Gift of Sadness

A child that never finds trust becomes an adult with no faith. Faith is not supposed to mean that you trust blindly out of fear. It is supposed to mean that you trust based on feeling. To someone who has forgotten how to *feel,* faith seems like a joke because it has no substance—no proof—it is not quantifiable. How can you teach faith to adults who don't trust their own feelings?

Adults in this condition go through the most unbelievable confusion as they freefall from their comfortable world of rationality into an untrustworthy and intangible world of feeling without thought. They don't trust their own inner voice that says they will be fine, because the last time it told them that, someone shamed or ridiculed them for being true to it.

This freefall for them is the ultimate loss of control, and they erupt inside with decades of hurt and rejection. Only the strongest and most willful can find the courage to trust once again in themselves and the Source. Try saying "I don't know" to yourself over and over, day after day, until you undermine your choking rationality.

As you awaken and become more sensitive, you will feel utter emptiness and desolation. But you have to go through it. The tremendous sadness in you is the heartbreak of your light body that has not been allowed to express or fulfill itself for most of your life—until now.

You sink to the very bottom, freaking out the entire way. Your body cries and cries, releasing its frustration and sorrow, and all of its impurities. You will lose weight down to the bone where even the marrow must be cleansed. Your friends and family will consider coming to get you, or try to offer you "professional" help.

But when you finally find the bottom and land on your back—staring up through the depths to the surface and the faint twinkling of the distant stars—a peace starts to run through you. Here is where you learn to see beyond your pain and sadness. Here is where you learn that life continues on beyond what you *thought* was the end.

"Sinking to the bottom" is learning to walk *through* fear. You will feel sick to your stomach. But the greatest thing about hitting the bottom is that you never again in your life have to be afraid of the unknown depths—you know exactly how far down the abyss goes.

Now you can see the bigger picture because you finally let go of everything you knew and let death swallow you. You didn't find death. You found *yourself*—your emotional past—buried in the dark depths that you closed off because somebody else hurt you. You rose up out of the former you.

Your arrogance practically killed you, and for what? To get back at someone for injuring you out of anger and pain? But you only hurt yourself. This is the lesson. This life is about you. You need to live for yourself. Make yourself perfect and enjoy yourself. You will never forget this lesson. Your longing and helpless wishing are replaced by silent determination.

Everybody must go through their own fire swamp or pit of despair in order to conquer fear. That's why it's a mythological archetype. It is a solo period of inner testing and courage, where one learns to face the demons and doubts within.

I remember the moment when I silently wished for death at the height of my own self-indulgence and pity. I knew implicitly that I only had to utter the words and it would've come to pass. But I didn't. I wasn't that stupid.

When you see the big picture, you realize that all is within your control. This is your creation, for better or for worse. You choose your partners and friends. You select which thoughts to make into reality, and you create with the energy of emotion. Now you can devote your energy to seeing how high you can go.

The Earth

I am thoroughly confused by the bumper stickers that read "Save the Earth." What kind of arrogance is that? Believe me, the Earth can take care of herself, and already does. The bumper sticker should read "Save the Humans," because when we pollute and pillage we are only destroying ourselves.

The Earth *allows* us to learn from our own stupidity and greed—she is our patient partner in this dream. But, as a sentient being, she will protect herself if she needs to. When we create extinctions in the animal kingdom, we only disrupt our own food chain—the animals know where they are going. When we tear down rain forests, new diseases appear. When we dump toxic waste into the ocean, it shows up in our fish. When we pollute the atmosphere with our gas guzzling and pesticides, we wind up with contaminated drinking water, asthma, birth defects, and all kinds of cancers. The Earth will be just fine. Many humans will not be so lucky.

Our physical bodies are of the Earth, and our light bodies

are from the stars. We vibrate according to the Earth and according to the heavens. We follow the moods of the Earth, and resonate according to its low frequencies. In the winter, we turn inside and long to hibernate and not be hurried. We are more quiet and reflective. In the summer, we spring outward with energy and delight, desiring to explore our physicality and revel in activity. Vibrating and uniting with the moods of the Earth creates harmony and power, and an enduring physicality.

Chakras

Each chakra is an entity, a being in its own right. Each has its own personality, its own rhythm, and its own strengths. Each has a favorite time of day or night, and each requires certain "foods" or energies. They can each be selfish, hoarding energy at the expense of the others out of fear and covetousness.

If you were shamed as a child when you connected to your light body via the third eye, or if people made fun of you for communing with the Source through your crown, then those chakras harbor fear and resentment and will have a tendency to keep energy away from the rest of the body in an attempt to make up for the hurt. Allow them the freedom they need and gently coax them to work with the rest.

Upon manifesting into the physical plane, you set up certain emotional or energetic impediments within your chakras to create restrictions in your life flow. These are your life lessons. If you go through life in a semiconscious state, these blocks will continue to impede your life flow and facilitate emotional and physical problems. In order to dismantle the blocks, you need to become conscious of them and conscious of the fear, or illusion, that is the block itself. This is the process of awakening.

The most direct way to approach any block is to face it in the moment. It sounds easy enough, but the reality is that you have to step out of whatever drama or fear you're smack dab in the middle of and stop everything—just stop. Stop talking, stop thinking, stop arguing, stop eating, stop moving, stop running away—stop, stop, stop. You are resisting the reality in the moment. Then, when you're all stopped, *listen*. Way deep inside, hidden beneath layer after layer, is a tiny whispering feeling that's telling you what you're afraid of. It's telling you what your illusion is. Listen to it. Change your behavior and your reactions to the illusion, *immediately*. Now the block begins to clear. You do this each time until it no longer exists.

Talking excessively, or the overuse of any chakra, is born of fear. It could be the fear of silence, or the fear of intimacy that comes from knowing someone so well that you can sit silently with them and not get squirmy, or the fear of not being thought highly of in a social situation if you are silent for too long. It's much more difficult to sit in a room with someone in silence. It allows you to be vulnerable, open. Talking is like armor, a deflection from the intimacy of silence. Talking wears out the brain.

Anytime you focus excessively on a particular chakra it creates an imbalance in your system, and it may require a whole day of rest to rectify it. Sometimes you need to go there. All right then. But just be aware of the subtleties.

If you are afraid for your physical health, you will overexercise. If you fear the loss of sex or its associated pleasures, you will indulge in it at the expense of your physical well-being. If you are afraid of not having enough power, then you will wield it excessively so that nobody takes advantage of you or thinks you're weak. If you are afraid of not being loved or that you're not worthy of love, you will become a bleeding heart, projecting your fear onto others, assuming that they need as much mothering as you do.

If you fear manifesting your creativity or Truth, you will babble on about anything just to clear the energy from your throat chakra. If your third eye is shut or barely open, you will question others ad nauseam in an attempt to understand from the outside what should be self-evident from your light body and intuition—the inside. If your crown is plugged up, you will think until your hair falls out, trying to access the Source with your physical brain and dastardly logic.

If one chakra develops ahead of the others, you will encounter and interact with your world primarily through that chakra. This is how you learn about, and mature, that chakra. If your heart chakra develops strength first, you may meet the world with too much love and be a bleeding heart, fussing over and apologizing for everybody else's difficulties. If your wiener chakra is the strongest, then you will meet people with your wiener at the expense of your heart. If it's your solar plexus, then your mode will be aggression and dominance without creativity. If it's your third eye, then your mode will be looking into everybody's potentiality regardless of their superficial presentation, and you will be thoroughly baffled when they are anything less than their ultimate potential.

The opposite is also true. If your solar plexus is your weakest or slowest to develop, then your interactions will be characterized by timidity or mousiness. If your third eye is lagging, then you will take people only at face value. If your sexual nature is slow to develop, then you may be seen as effeminate. These factors will encourage the protraction or retraction of body parts in your physical posturing, too—sticking out your pelvis, chest, or head while the rest of you trails behind. If you allow your chakras to develop in their own way and in their own time, they will eventually all be in balance and you will meet the world with fullness.

Power is the activation and *incorporation* of your lower three chakras. This doesn't mean that you run around pursuing physical indulgences or sex and power *over* others. It means that you ignite and perfect your physical vehicle, creational energy, and power, and then use that energy to bolster your upper chakras in your pursuit of evolution and your multidimensional birthright.

Chakra	Base	Sexual	Solar Plexus
Possible Indulgences or Lower Chakra Functions (including too much or too little —referring to repression of that chakra's energy)	Sensuality (of the five senses), food, anal sex, material posses-sions, overdevelop-ment of physical body at expense of light body, athletics or exercise, complete physical immersion with no seeing ability.	Sex, masturbation, sensuality, self-confidence, tyranny.	Power over people or animals, money, frustration, anger, self-evolution, self-aggrandizement, attachment (not enough reliance on your own power).
Associated Fears	Fear of bodily harm, fear of illness, fear of unleashing physical force or developing physical prowess, fear of dominance or submission, fear of physical life.	Fear of sex or sex-ual advances, fear of sexual power, fear of creational abilities, fear of intimate physical contact, fear of water, fear of inti-macy.	Fear of power, fear of loss of power, fear of loss of sta-tus, fear of getting what you want, fear of action, fear of getting squished.
Higher Chakra Functions	Perfection of the physical vehicle to support and mani-fest higher chakra functions and light body creativity.	Sexual chakra energy used to bolster upper chakras and fires, especially third eye.	Combined with heart and upper chakra leads to power and force with joy and vision—will and eternity.

Heart	Throat	Third Eye	Crown
Worry, crying, emotional dependence, gentleness, sadness (grief is in the lungs); heart in stand-alone mode uses love as excuse for getting attention.	Talking, self-expression as an excuse for irresponsibility, extroversion, creativity as an excuse for slothfulness, listening, money.	Intuition, clarity, passivity, illusion, seeing at the expense of doing.	Other worlds and realities (at the expense of the rest of your physical body), rationality, thinking.
Fear of joy, fear of loss of love, fear of affection, fear of not being liked.	Fear of expression (not just talking or singing, but all creativity), fear of speaking out against or for things or people, lack of expression of emotion, fear of looking stupid.	Fear of intuition, fear of insanity, fear of loss of identity, fear of action, fear of responsibility.	Fear of physicality, fear of losing what you know (your rationality), fear of letting go of your past, fear of spontaneous action based solely on feeling-tones.
Love coupled with power, force, vision, and eternity.	Creative aggression in the manifestation of order; creativity and expression used for promotion of the world of the light body.	Vision coupled with action and the fearlessness of the lower chakras, intuition, soul-based feelings or expression, harmony and communion between your physical body and light body, dreaming.	Perfection. The Source. No identification with the self—you are the flame—the eternal moment—there is no more self-reflection!

If someone attempts to make you afraid, disengage your thoughts and fears, and notice to which of your chakras that person is sending the fearful energy. Not only can you then release that energy into the ground and render the other person harmless and flustered, but you will also know precisely what fears that person is ruled by since that is the same chakra attacked in you. Or, you can use the other's energy to fuel a higher chakra in yourself and send a positive message back to the person—perhaps a message of evolution.

Each chakra is an umbilical cord between your light body and your physical body, with each chakra corresponding to a specific power and related internal organ(s) and gland(s). The important thing here is not to get overly focused on the details, but rather spend your energy encouraging and unleashing the potential of each chakra. If there is discomfort in your body, take note of the area and see if you have imposed any limitations on the energy from that chakra.

Chakra blockages often plug up on the back of the physical body—knots, lumps, or stiffness. The *unmanifested* energy has not been *brought forward*. It has been shoved back behind the energy center that is not being allowed to express. The reduction of the flow of energy through a chakra and its associated organs and muscles caused by repression is what creates the retention of heavy metals or toxins in those areas. Detoxification and a releasing of these impurities, especially from the brain, creates a type of hysteria and panic in the body.

Our society is crammed with half-assed and fearful examples of teachers with completely unbalanced chakra systems. The majority of them have overly developed heart chakras coupled with repressed lower chakras. A well-developed chakra system sees a rigorous development of each chakra and then a balancing and ordering with the purpose of seeing and understanding all realities here.

The lower three chakras must be developed and utilized. The physical must be nurtured and tended to, the sexual energy must be understood and ignited, and power must

Chakra	Associated Organs, Glands, and Areas of the Body
Base	Kidneys, adrenals, perineum, anus, descending colon.
Sexual	Reproductive organs and glands, pelvis, navel area, lower back.
Solar Plexus	Liver, intestines, stomach.
Heart	Heart and thymus, lungs, area between shoulder blades.
Throat	Neck, thyroid, upper back and base of neck, ears.
Third Eye	Center of head, hypothalamus, pituitary, pineal, forehead.
Crown	The swan wings or cortex of the brain (the cortex is supposed to be a sensory organ, not a rational computer), top of head.

thrive. If these are not functioning wholly and properly, then you will wind up like most of the current love-and-flowers gurus with their bleeding and overindulgent heart chakras, effeminate representations, and impotent messages.

Fear of passion and power have made this the norm. Because our history is replete with examples of leaders who have developed *only* the lower three chakras, we have over-reacted by repressing the lower three and overdeveloping the heart, throat, and mind. But this is not correct either. *All* must be developed and incorporated in order to evolve completely.

The energy of each chakra can be developed and matured by living and doing what you feel—the feeling always comes before the conclusion or rationalization. If you desire to evolve to your ultimate potential, then the energy of each chakra needs to be free to roam at will throughout your body and other chakras. Practice glowing each chakra by focusing on it lightly until it radiates, and then release the energy and feel it flow throughout your body. The only way to achieve this is to will it into existence by practicing it over and over. There is no method except pure intention, a clear mind, and unwavering persistence and focus.

When the light body is one hundred percent anchored to the base chakra, then people instinctively know that you are immovable and unshakable, absolutely solid in yourself, and they will not mess with you. This kind of grounding also makes you very arousing to others, since your energetic stance pulls them into their lower chakras.

Your sexual energy should not be restricted to your second chakra; it must be allowed to roam freely. The energy of your will or solar plexus must be allowed to mingle with your heart energy to create a power based on joy.

If you bring your sexual energy up and it encounters a blocked solar plexus, you may become unpleasantly aggressive with sexual overtones, or become completely withdrawn and intimidated by women if you're a former Catholic. Or, if that energy encounters a frustrated throat chakra, you may become a loud drunkard. If it finds a dormant third eye, your head may go fuzzy and be filled with pornographic thoughts. Understanding how energy moves (or is blocked) within each of your chakras is a process that can take many years. Be patient and, above all, be *observant*.

The brain is supposed to be a sensory organ—a feeling chakra in its own right. Thinking is its lower function, or the way in which it hoards energy like the other chakras. Thinking can be indulged in at the expense of the rest of the body just like sex, power, or talking can be. If you wake up slowly in the morning and just enjoy the way that your body feels after a good sleep and some vivid dreams, then you will catch a glimpse of the fuller functionality of your brain chakra—spontaneity based on zero rationality or prejudgment.

Fall in love with your physical body and its perfection, and your sexual nature. Fall in love with your power, will, and self-expression. Fall in love with your consciousness, the Source, and your creative aggression. Put love, lust, and passion together with power, awareness, and unlimited physicality and see what you can manifest.

The chakras are incomplete energies by themselves. The overdevelopment of any one chakra creates a brittle power that is easily injured or thrown off balance. The rest of the system is weakened. But together they form the totality—the light body made physical.

Flying

I feel thoroughly exhilarated, running down the dark street in a quiet urban neighborhood just outside an industrial district. I am trying to get up the speed or momentum to fly across the housetops, which are all tinted a moonlit gray. I start rotating my arms like a locomotive, faster and faster. I reach out, enlarging the rotating circles, and start gaining speed. Sparks flash. I increase the speed and size of the circles until there is a blinding flash and I black out.

I come to on one of the moonlit gray rooftops. I have some kind of balloon or floatation device strapped around my waist. I am able to bounce off the roof and then down the street, leaping and accelerating. I'm still not flying yet, but I am getting very close.

I look up and see large black meteor fragments with glowing red embers moving quickly across the sky. I know that if I attach myself to one it will help me fly, so I jump up and fly to one, and it carries me away.

3

Relationships

I gently tapped on her bedroom door the next morning. I heard her make that little sound that said it was okay to come in. She was still in bed. The sweetness of her rumpled hair and those eyes that were always so happy to see me looked back and my heart almost broke.

"C'mon, Sweet Pea. It's time," I said shakily. "Put on your clothes and let's go downstairs."

She looked confused, but got dressed. Her morning smell made everything so homey. I took her hand and we walked downstairs and sat by a window with a little sunlight streaming through. I looked at her.

"I realized this morning that I am holding you captive," I said, my throat starting to get hard. I started to cry, but then suddenly laughed and smiled gently at her. Then I cried some more. "I realized that I am afraid, and that your anger and frustration have manifested more because of this."

Some more tears fell. She started to cry, too.

"Despite my strength and desire to walk into the Unknown, I still live in this world and in relationship to the world. Would I be the best that I can be if I didn't face *all* of my fears, including my fears with you? I am holding you back with my fear. I don't know that we can resolve things right now, but it's time to begin."

We held each other, sobbing and shaking. I could hardly talk. I stuttered and choked on my words.

"I would like to thank you for being patient with me and giving me the chance to grow and become a man. But we *have* to create something new here, something we've never tried or even heard about. We have to allow each other to go, and come back! That is usually where all the pain is, that we never leave the door open. We always cut everything off in our fear and deny affection. We can't do that here.

"We sought security with each other in our old habits, but they are just dead patterns with no spontaneity and no joy. They are our fears trying desperately to hold on to what used to bring us happiness. But that's just it—what *used* to bring us happiness. We are growing, and we have to go forward. Then we will find a relationship based on affection and not fear. Our relationship is dying. But I want to save it by facing my fears and by saying these things to you. I know that you see it, too, and that you are angry and disappointed with me for allowing this stagnation to creep in and make us both sour inside. The Source wants us to move forward. We want to move forward."

The room filled with sadness and fear as she looked at me. I had never before been with someone for whom I felt so much constant affection. It only made it that much harder.

"How come it feels like you're going away?" she asked, her tears falling freely.

"I'm not going away, sweetheart. I'll still be here tomorrow. It feels like I'm going away because your fear of losing me makes you pull inside. You only know how to open yourself all the way and spill all your energy, or pull in and shut everything down."

She nodded and held my hands, caressing my fingers.

"I'm trying to show you how to just keep the affection flowing without trying to use me to fill yourself up, and the same for me. We need some time to ourselves—I need time to figure out how to get what I want. I need to go wherever and do whatever without jerking you around until I can see past the limitations I've put on myself because I was afraid of losing you."

"I want you to know that I want this to work, no matter how long it takes," I said, as I looked into her eyes. "We need to work together while we are apart—we can't let fear stand in our way."

We held each other for a long time, sobbing off and on. It felt so good to be with her. No one else had ever walked as far with me as she had. Her affection was so pure. I loved her dearly.

"You know it's the right thing," she finally said.

And right then I knew it was.

What Is a Relationship?

You can seek outside yourself for experience, or you can search within yourself and eventually meet others who do the same. Seeking outside yourself is necessary when you need clarity, when you need a mirror to help you see what you are blind to. Another person can be of great assistance in helping you to see the nuances of attachment, indulgence, self-pity, and arrogance. They can also become eternal friends if you both journey toward awareness together. You may discover that even though you have a tremendous love for each other, what's exciting is that you really *like* each other's company— you are lovers *and* best friends. Never underestimate the strength of your feelings for a person.

You can apply your lessons from your relationships to your experience with yourself and your relationship to the Source. It's a never-ending journey, for there are thousands of energies and potential relationships outside our own world. Eventually, you will prefer to spend more and more time alone, until such time when you find others who are very clear and filling themselves constantly with light. The constant presence of others not of this state can actually be very saddening and annoying, like a little hysterical barking dog. I know that sounds horrible, but their lessons are their own, and there's nothing you can do about their journey. You must have your own.

If we all work on perfecting ourselves in earnest, then there will exist the possibility of a coming together. Ultimately, we all seek to unite, not so that we can lose our individuality in each other or in the collective, but so that we can work together in our power to grow and create.

Relationships are not Band-Aids for your personal deficiencies. You still have to do your homework. Your problems will not go away because she is here. In fact, they will be magnified. She is a mirror for your misperceptions. You get to see yourself more clearly because of her.

Symbiosis always creates energetic limitations, and not just in human relationship. If you can't work well in a relationship with another human being, how will you interact with the myriad energetic realities that you have yet to uncover? The world of relationship is a doorway into your hidden fears and secret agendas, a way for you to learn how to relate to any energy. Here is where you get to see your limitations up close.

Everything is a relationship. So becoming a hermit to avoid the world of relationships is a fallacy. Time alone is crucial for reflecting and recapitulating your contributions, or lack thereof, in any relationship. But it is only temporary. Then you get plopped right back into another relationship—or the same one.

By yourself, you are perfect. In relationship, you suck, and your relationships always end in misery and failure. How do you behave, and in what ways do you react, when surrounded by anger, fear, or sadness? Do you allow her fear to push you face-first into your own, or do you run away from her and into the arms of another to avoid the challenge? By relating to another without fear, your affection is always alive—it never needs to be rekindled.

Living Together
Men and women should not live together. Actually, every

person should have their own primary space, and *then* share space with others when appropriate. Sleeping in the same bed with a woman night after night can easily lead to exhaustion. You will quickly find out if you are with her because you value her friendship or because she has nice boobs. Live in your own place and visit when you are strong.

If you live with a woman, you will eventually stop having sex with her. She will become more your best friend and confidante, and you may seek romances outside your home. The desire not to be bothered with sex in your personal space is what triggers this.

Men and women want their homes to be places of quiet where they can unwind, relax, be themselves, and not have to be on guard. Having a woman in your house changes that. It is fun for a while, but then you want your space back. You don't want to have to be on guard in case your partner jumps you, or disrupts your silence or train of thought. You don't want someone always focused on you. This is why sexual affairs are so popular—you don't have to bring them home with you. The hot sex stays outside the house, so that you can walk away from it when you're done.

Dependence and Attachment

Dependence and attachment are present when you are busy thinking of ways to keep your partner happy and interested in you. If you are worried that your partner will forget about you or find somebody better the moment you leave the room, then your self-esteem is lacking.

If you make yourself the best that you can be, then *you* will know it. And if she leaves you for another, then obviously she is not aware enough to see what you have accomplished and needs to go and find out. The norm is to attempt to find the missing pieces of yourself in someone else. Needing another person is not love. The only thing you need is the Source.

You cannot help or save others. It's their deal all the way.

You can only be a mirror for them, too. If they're into grow-ing, then they might actually listen to you. The same goes for you and whether or not you listen to your partner. Partners have an uncanny ability to tell you perfectly what your prob-lem is, while not having a clue about themselves. But that's what a mirror does.

If you use pleasure as the means to fill yourself up from the outside, then you will always be searching for more pleas-ure. You will never be satisfied because there is always some-one better looking, better built, more sexual, sweeter, funnier, cockier, and more willing. The fear of never having the pleas-ure again is what makes you want it more. Before you are done with one, you are looking for another. It also makes you cling more tightly to what you have in the meantime. It is a trap, an endless cycle. Let go of the quick fix and do your homework. Learn to fill yourself up and you will finally be satisfied.

If you or your partner are afraid to make "mistakes" around each other, and so avoid doing new things or things that make you look bad, then there is fear of failure and attachment tangled together. One of you will always be afraid to live your life or do what your impulses tell you because you might do the "wrong" thing, or appear weak trying. If you appear weak, you are in danger of being replaced by someone stronger. Then fear surrounds the heart, choking off self-love and, therefore, the ability to love anyone else. Fear strangles the love that the heart is trying to communicate.

Never hold back a person with your fear. If you see fear in your relationship, walk through it until it dissipates. Take your time so as not to miss the subtleties along the way. Even if you have to let your partner go for now, know that your bravery has made you a better man and the world a better place. We're all in this together, and you can be sure that you will grow and find many rewards every time you challenge yourself.

"I have to go away from you because I have allowed your disbelief to infect me. I can barely see the light that beckons me anymore. Every day I struggle amidst this darkness to keep not only my head above water, but yours as well. You are no longer my partner—you are my liability. Everything I do to further myself, you tear down because of your fear of losing me—you want me to stay put."

Some believe that love is attachment—cuddly, snuggly, insecure, and stagnant. This is the belief that you and your partner are too incompetent and scared of life to face head on and conquer. So the two of you create a little bubble-world to feel safe in. It can work for you if you see it for what it is and evolve from children into adults—repair your past hurts and move on. Then the two of you create vibrancy, power, and confidence in yourselves and each other.

The severing of attachment leaves a big void in your gut, a gaping hole. You will be feverish on and off for days or many weeks, depending on the severity of your attachment and dependence. Your stomach will rumble, you will lose your appetite, and food will make you queasy. The best remedy is hot meat broth and light snacks. Get some kind of exercise and drive around. It will heal in time.

Allowing

Others have their own consciousness, and they can do whatever they want with it. You do what you need. Spend less time judging and more time living. Even if your intuitions about your partner are dead-on, there's no need to throw any condescension into the mix. She is what she is. You go and do what you have to.

Doubt and Fear

If you worry about your partner's safety when she leaves the house, then you doubt her abilities and your own. If you truly believe in your partner and want her to blossom into the fullness of herself, then you will stop creating fear for her within yourself. You will trust her to be the best of herself and leave her alone so that she can do that. Don't ever doubt her; give her the gift of your belief and confidence in her intelligence and desire for self-fulfillment.

And don't tell her to "be careful," either. If you do, you are implying that she is an idiot with a death wish. Where's your faith, man? Maybe you secretly hope that she *will* have an accident so that it will be even more obvious that she needs you, and then you will get to take care of her. Or maybe you're just afraid that she will never come back.

Don't try to force your partner to adopt your fears. Keep yourself from forcing your fear onto her; then she will always be a reminder to you that you have a fear that you have not dealt with yet.

Anger

Don't be an indiscriminate asshole with your anger and frustration and take it out on your partner or anyone else who's close by. Take it out on its source—you. If you bring home anger and frustration, then it's your problem. Your partner is not your personal punching bag or scapegoat. Take responsibility for yourself and your own creations.

Possession

Fear and possession are so very subtle. To want to own the rights to someone else's happiness or to expect always to be the only source of her greatest joy *is* possession. The ultimate difficulty is to be completely happy and full by yourself. But the ultimate joy is to accept the challenge of loving without fear of loss or conditions.

You seek to possess people, animals, and things because you are trying to fill yourself up from the outside. But if you succeed in being truly happy in yourself and by yourself, then you will truly be happy when others are happy without you.

When you are happy in yourself and she is happy in herself, and neither one of you needs anything from the other, then you freely *choose* to spend time with each other because you feel real joy together and not the fake joy that comes with terms and conditions. The joy that has conditions is based on fear—"I will only love you this much if you can give back an equal amount of love or praise or attention," or "You had an orgasm. Where's mine?" True affection expects nothing in return and has no conditions.

We all want unconditional love, but are incapable of and unwilling to work toward giving unconditional love. If you are covetous and stingy with your energy and love, you will always be in want for energy and love—and money. You will always have a silent expectation that your partner should fill you up when you are not full. What happens when you get two empty people? Look out!

Dominance

Typically, one partner dominates the other. The energy of the subservient one dribbles out of their second and third chakras on a regular basis upon surrender of power. This is a huge turn-off to the dominant one, who will eventually reject the subservient one for another. For a relationship to evolve, there must be equality and a pliable tension between the two. Both must remain in control of their energy. This is impossible if one desires to be "taken care of" by the other and has not learned energetic self-responsibility and chakra maturation. This imbalance is indicated by one partner being too available, or always waiting for the other to decide.

Compromise

Never compromise for the sake of a relationship. In a relationship that is not based on attachment, need, or expectations, there is no requirement to stunt your growth in order to give another person a false sense of security. If your partner requires this of you in order to feel like you care about her and her fears, tell her that you are not interested in having her fears imposed on you so that she can feel better about her cowardice. We all have fears to face. We don't need to carry someone else's baggage for them.

To weaken yourself for another in order to comfort her does neither one of you any good. You must always be in your strength, and that strength can either give her the confidence that she can do it, too, or it will push her and her self-doubt away.

Coercion

"I open myself to you, and you use this as a chance to try to bring me down to your level. You use my openness and my desire to help you understand as an opportunity to plant the seeds of doubt. I am addressing that part of you that knows what it's doing, even though you are not conscious of it yet. I am speaking directly to it, calling its bluff, and telling it that I will not play its game or allow it to curse me.

"Sometimes you cry because you're seeking attention. Sometimes you cry and get upset because you're healing. I have to discern which is which, because one needs a friend and the other needs a kick in the ass. Now is not the time for you to stop working because you believe that you've done enough for today. No! Now is the only time there is."

Emotional Pain and Sadness

Emotional pain is not to be avoided. It is to be welcomed. Pain indicates illusion and energetic confusion. It shows you your own myopia and attachment. It tells you where the blocks are. Drama demands attention and is a supreme waste of energy. I am so sick of endings.

I stand at the edge of the waterfall, the furious water rushing madly toward me. I breathe deeply, searching for that stillness that keeps me from being swept away to my own death. Her fears grow stronger by the second, each falling tear trying desperately to pull me into the swirling darkness of her mind. But I have been there before, and I no longer need to go there. I watch in my own silent desperation as she flails about hopelessly, searching for something to keep her from going under. All I can do now in my lesson is hold steady and show her my strength and will to survive. She looks up for just a moment into my eyes. I wink.

Crying and sadness arise because your brain's logic denies what is coming directly from her and being registered in your heart and other energy centers; you have an expectation of her that is not a reality. Crying and sadness are confusion over reality. Your heart and chakras have direct communication with her. But your expectations about what you want from her to satisfy your needs close off your ability to hear what your chakras are telling you about her current state.

When you are afraid of losing somebody you love, the habit is to lash out against her, subtly or not so subtly, to drive her further away. It is a mistaken belief that it is less painful to lose somebody who is mean in return, or who has been driven further away. But the sadness will always come back to you. You may have temporarily desensitized yourself, but your body *always* remembers.

Permanence

Relationships last as long as they need to. There is no need to force anything. If you sever a relationship, you can never go back. If you do, you will quickly realize why you left in the first place. The core of the problem will not change overnight unless one of you takes a magic pill, and they are hard to find.

There are other ways to leave a relationship that don't involve devastating heartbreak and permanent endings. If you still love the person, then separate for a time so that you can both work on things individually. This only works, however, if both of you have reached a state of development where you want to spend time by yourselves and don't immediately run out in your fear and get involved in another relationship.

Habits give the illusion of permanence, but they are dead patterns of speech or action with no spontaneity and no feeling of joy. They are your fears trying desperately to cling to the security that used to bring you happiness. But now you have outgrown those needs—you have evolved—and it's time to allow yourself to move forward before the bitterness creeps in.

There are times when you both know a relationship is

over, but neither one of you wants to be the jerk who ends it. So you become a different kind of jerk and try to drive your partner away by doing things she hates. Grow up! Be energetically bold and face your fear. Tell her and show her with your heart *open* that you still have affection for her but would like to be on your way. And if she's the one who's being the jerk, then with love and humor call her on her crappy behavior and suggest a parting of ways.

Nothing need ever end. You can still be connected, still be close. The pain is in the ending. Why end it? Then you lose a friend as if she had died. This is an immature way of transitioning in your life. Leave it open-ended. You don't need to push out of your life everyone you can't control. This takes more courage because the love is now out of your control; your vulnerability can come and go as it pleases. But you are brave for allowing her and your love for her to be free.

Love is love. It doesn't mean that you have to live with the person you love, or that you have to marry her or commit to seeing her every other week. Don't screw it up or mangle it because of fear. No expectation should ever destroy love. Love is eternal, but only if you both *allow* it to be. Love is forever, but only where both desire eternity for themselves. Love is magnificent, but only if it is not brought down to live in our pettiness. Love is endless when there is no fear. I choose to share love with all. Who will do the same? I love you.

The Mirror

I am standing in a small bathroom in somebody's house, looking at a dental mirror with a brown wooden handle. It keeps vibrating in my hand and making a low-pitched crackling sound, something like an old radio. A teenage girl, Bonnie, is helping me. She is very sweet and present. Everything is extremely vivid.

Then the dental mirror somehow tunes into the frequency of the stars through the open window, and other life forces start coming through the mirror into the bathroom. The room fills with crackling static electricity, and the presence charges my spine and solar plexus. My hair stands straight up as the electricity frizzles through my skull.

I wake up suddenly in my bed, chills gushing up and down my spine, and sweeping in waves all over my body. I look around the room for a presence, but see none. After a few minutes, the waves subside. I shudder one last time. Then I look up through the open skylight. Three bright stars twinkle at me.

Sharing

What is the difference between buying a 60-acre plot of land *with* your woman and each of you buying your *own* 30-acre parcel, side by side? Can you feel the difference? Buying two individual side-by-side parcels gives each of you a sense of accomplishment and freedom in your own space. You are free to happily be the king and queen of your own castles. You are the masters of your own destinies by each manifesting your strongest reality, side by side. Then you can share or be alone, depending on your mood or need.

Do not feel threatened by your partner's need to be alone. Alone time is puttering time, downtime, introspective introversion, quiet time, mindlessness, formlessness, a chance to relate only with the Source, recapitulation, meditation, sloppy laziness, pick and scratch-the-crack time, greasy eye-moco time, feel the flow time, search for new horizons and manifest your dream time. Here is where we can look and see if we are following the voice of our light bodies accurately, or if we are clear in our interpretations and feelings. We can completely zone out without anyone watching or judging, practice singing or belly dancing, try on new ways of looking at energy without feeling the weight of another's paradigm or system, or stain our underwear with a heartfelt blast.

Stubborn Lessons

Everybody is stubborn and pigheaded—that's how we learn. We hang onto our bafflingly ridiculous ways regardless of the evidence stacked against us until we *see it* and *feel it* for ourselves. We must have our experiences for ourselves, and *no one* can enlighten us until we have *lived* them.

The struggle to resist Truth when given by *others* is the struggle of your consciousness to live its own lessons. It creates in the shadow of the light body, the Master Creator, and struggles to find its identity. It fights so hard because as a child it was beaten down and trampled on by other negative egos. It was shamed, ridiculed, and taught to *ignore* the Truth of your light body. Each person needs to live *exactly* as they feel it, regardless. This is how a person learns from injuries and their own lack of confidence, and then stands back up.

An ego that was bruised and shamed in childhood has to do things in its own way and in its own time in order to rebuild its confidence. It will purposefully reject *all* advice or suggestions—good or bad—that keep it from feeling that it is in control and doing its job. That ego wants to be very sure that no one else can take any credit for its achievements because that would negate its accomplishments. So don't feel rejected or let your own ego get bruised—just get out of her way.

No two human beings are exactly alike, and each has a unique blend of confusion that needs to be seen past through individual experience. A soul mate is not someone who travels with you side by side through each and every adventure and lesson. Everybody's seasons vary. We all need to self-create and make it on our own, with the encouragement and support of the other. Build her up in her desire to do it her own way.

Besides, you don't change people by cramming your beliefs down their throats. You change them by changing yourself. Now they can follow your example—if they choose to. The end point is the same, but the path never is.

Openness and Vulnerability

At some point with your partner, you finally feel secure enough, and then you proceed to open up the secret vault of your deepest emotions, dreams, and secrets. The two of you express and reveal your innermost truths and weaknesses. There is a deep level of trust, or maybe stupidity, and with that trust comes fear. Somebody who knows your weaknesses has the ability to hurt you very deeply if you don't do what she asks you to do. She has the knowledge of how to manipulate you by using your fears and weaknesses as leverage. She could expose you or ridicule your deepest feelings. She could also help you to grow.

Now you feel vulnerable. *Now,* more than ever, you want

to control her, watch her and know her every movement. You desire to control the potential release of your top-secret information to the enemy. You watch her minutely, looking for signs that she might be working for the other side. Your fear leads you to attempt to limit your partner, because by limiting her you can minimize the potential damage. You want to limit her like you limit yourself.

You have limited your self-expression. You have learned to lock your deepest truths and feelings deep, deep inside. You learned this when you were younger, when one of your teachers, parents, or peers shamed you for showing any signs of life—any feelings, moods, sensitivity, faith or hope, intuition, love, pure joy, *individuality*, creativity, or power. Or someone may have shamed you because you stated perfect Truth when it was not welcome. You were absolutely shocked to your core that someone could embarrass you so completely for being so *honest*. How could they squash what was so pure? But you showed them—you locked it up and threw away the key. These people had no right to, or respect for, the real deal. So as far as you were concerned, they could take their petty miscreant lives and shove them up their collective ass.

But now you are an adult and heading toward energetic maturity. You don't want any limitations inside or out, and you don't want any more fear in your life. You want to be cocky and fearless, and express yourself regardless of the jeers of the faceless paupers. By doing this, you eliminate the need for secrecy and concealment—your life becomes an open book. You have no limitations on yourself, inside or out, and so there is no need for you to limit or control anyone else because you are *close to everyone*.

Now you and your partner are free because there is nothing that threatens you. You have nothing to hide, and you have no need to be covetous, jealous, or possessive. You stand in front of others without fear and express yourself boldly because you know it's what everyone needs to do. You put yourself on display for all to see.

Arrogance and Self-Esteem

Your arrogance may lead you to the false belief that she will fail without you—that she's too weak or childlike. But that arrogance is really a fear that she may not *need* you—that she may go out and be fine on her own—maybe even do *better* without you. If that happened, could you let her return? Or would you be shattered on realizing that you aren't as great as you thought you were? She did better without you! Why does she need you?

Did you use her to bolster your own confidence, the two of you believing the whole time that you were some magnanimous being sent to care for the helpless people of the world? But now it becomes clear that this is not the case. You have to find your own power without anybody else's discipleship to boost your morale. You have to fill yourself up from the inside by working your ass off to establish a beefy connection to the Source. Now, if she returns, beaming with her success and confident in her abilities, you will be truly happy for her, and the two of you can begin again in a relationship based on equality and joy instead of symbiosis and fear.

Growing Up

There are probably only two people in this world who have had perfect childhoods with perfect parents and perfect teachers. The rest of us grew up in the ghetto of life and were eventually scarred by some ignorant fool who had good intentions but little self-awareness. This scarring stunted your effortless progression from child to adult, and left you somewhat incomplete and hurt. Now, as a deformed adult, you are expected to go out and interact with others without mangling them.

If you've been in a relationship and suddenly started talking to each other like little kids with cutesy pet names, now you know why. You have found a safe place to go back to that scarring moment and try to work through some of your confusion and pain. You are looking to grow up.

Rarely in our society do people have the chance to mature *within* a relationship. With our parents, we still call them "Mom" and "Dad"—even as adults—and we try to keep our mouths shut or not rock the boat too much at family gatherings out of respect for their status. It's a pleasant enough formality, but it doesn't teach us about coming into our own and *evolving* the energy of the relationship from "parent and child" to "partners and friends."

Along comes a relationship, and you're still deformed. What to do? Well, you step down a few decades to work through the deformity, and then attempt, *without any prior experience,* to mature within the relationship. You attempt to energetically develop your chakras, your mind, your body, and your avenues of communication with someone who's also fishing in the dark. This is a real challenge. Your tendency will be to dump her and go find someone else the moment it doesn't go the way you want it to. But if you can take the time to understand your fears and motivations, speak your feelings clearly, listen and understand where she's at, and work peacefully as friends who both desire to manifest the Source, then you will find a way to grow up together. Tear down the old patterns and take it to the next level.

Multiple Relationships, or When One Partner Isn't Enough Drama for You

When I was a child, if I stated out loud that Ralph was my best friend, it would make my other friends jealous, and then they would all fight with each other to be my new best friend. But then we all grew up and realized it was alright to have many friends, and now we all get along just fine.

The same thing is true about relationships. We just need to grow up and see past our fear of loss and our desire to pit one person against another.

Every relationship is separate, and should be given your complete attention and affection. If you choose to have more than one partner, don't ever compare them to each other. Each person in your life deserves the fullness of you, is unique, and should never be judged according to how she measures up to another. This is not about who's better or stronger or sexier— it's about your relationship to another aspect of the Source.

Each person that you encounter and have a connection with provides you with a different reflection of yourself. In other words, you see other aspects of yourself more clearly in your interactions with various people. And you share the lessons you learn from these reflections with all your partners. Being open to new relationships brings constant challenge into your life and keeps you from getting cozy in your isolated world. Your partner (and you, too) should be grateful to, and not afraid of, other people. Other people help us grow into the fullness of ourselves.

And these relationships do *not* have to involve sex.

Motion or Stagnation

Perhaps it is my desire to be stable or at peace that is my illusion. Perhaps I am really looking for constant motion and eternal change. Is that why I always seek new faces and new places? *I will never be settled.* I will always be transforming, evolving—off on a new adventure. I see that I seek not eternal stability or rest, but rather eternal peace *within* eternal motion—not stasis but evolution—rest within motion. I am a man of change, a catalyst to myself and others. I am the eye within the hurricane.

An erroneous belief that I embraced for a very long time was that I needed total rest and stillness in my life. In trying to achieve this state, I resisted all motion. In other words, I forced myself to sit still when I needed to move. The diseases and exhaustion that I had during this time were not caused because I needed more rest, but because I had been using up my strength *resisting* motion.

It takes more energy to resist motion in a fear-driven attempt to be still than it does to flow with the motion. I became a stick-in-the-mud and created additional friction and stress for all involved. The resistance of motion and its result-ing frustration can lead to diseases of *stagnation*, such as rashes, candidiasis, fungus, hemorrhoids, clogged or hardened arteries, gallstones, liver problems, kidney stones, halitosis, and heart attacks. Even diseases that appear to be diseases of excess, such as obesity, alcoholism, or chronic fatigue, are ulti-mately diseases caused by stagnant or repressed emotional energy.

The resistance of motion is the same as resisting change. I resist change in order to protect what I have. I've been trying to give myself and my partner a false sense of security through stagnation—a false appearance of *permanence*. But beneath that façade is utter turmoil.

I have been resisting my own creative power while seek-ing that illusion of rest within nonmovement, instead of seek-ing a meditative Zen joy within motion. How blind have I been? Was this born out of some fear? A fear of loss perhaps? A fear that change and motion might lead me away from her? It's the fear that if I change this way and she changes that other way, we will come apart. And so I try to force my partner to change according to *my plan*. This becomes the source of end-less arguments and friction until we eventually run away from each other to continue our individual evolutions on our own or with another.

Our friendships—as opposed to sexual relationships—are often far less restrictive and allow us to come and go as we please, to spend time with others without fear of losing our friend. Our sexual relationships would last longer if they were fluid friendships based not on fear of loss, but on joy and the desire to play as we evolve on our individual paths.

How many times have we said (or heard said), "She slows me down," "I give things up for her," or "I don't go surfing anymore because she's afraid I might get hurt," only to find ourselves feeling resentful toward our partner for making us give things up! And then we require our partner to give something up for us *in return* to make us feel better about our suffering, safe in our desire to please the other while denying ourselves. This is a slow death of self-starvation, the ultimate illusion of self-sacrifice that always leads to some kind of dramatic and resentful conclusion.

To continue that dance out of fear of loss and call it *commitment* leads to ugliness, disaster, and self-annihilation. We all need to come and go as we please, without fear, without self-denial. The love is always there, is it not, unless we ruin it by bottling up so much anger and resentment that we finally explode, attack our partner, and break up?

Intimacy

Real intimacy is the connection of two light bodies without the interference of perception. It is usually only glimpsed in intercourse. It is only glimpsed because the main focus is only on the second chakra. But when you learn to allow your sexual energy to flow above your baser desire, it flows up to your sixth chakra—your third eye. Sexual love becomes third-eye love, the kind where you touch your foreheads together and feel your hearts open. Here's where you find those deep, bonding hugs, the kind that dispel fear and tension, make things warm and snuggly, lighten the mood, lift both hearts, and show that there is tremendous affection. And when there's that kind of affection, the thoughts and divisions are absent. Now the chance for a communion of souls exists, both awake and asleep.

One time I was eating lunch at work across from a middle-aged woman that I was attracted to but barely knew. She was ultra-religious, and quite possibly a virgin waiting for a husband. We had been making small talk and flirting lightly.

I was looking down at my food when I realized that she was staring at me. I looked up at her, fully expecting her to look away. But she held my gaze and smiled. Everything came to a screeching halt. I was spellbound. We went way beyond the accepted time for two strangers to stare at each other.

Then, unexpectedly, our light bodies came out of our

eyes, met in the center of the lunchroom table, and then went *into* each other. It was more powerful and steamy than if we had suddenly stripped and had sex on the table. It lasted for almost a full minute. Then her ultra-religious perception kicked in and she threw her lunch back into her bag and raced off toward the bathroom, glancing back at me one more time. She was blushing as if she had just shown me her genitals and then suddenly remembered that we were supposed to be two strangers sitting in the break room at work.

Another time, at a different job, I was in the employee area with a group of coworkers. We were all looking at something in a newspaper. A woman that I was attracted to was standing to my left, and the other employees were behind us. Suddenly, I noticed that the woman was staring at me. I turned and looked at her, and she continued staring. I felt our light bodies merge very gently, but I could tell by the faraway look in her eyes that she was not conscious of what was happening. Yet she did not break the connection.

She stared at me for so long that a friend of hers who was also interested in me finally blurted out in a shocked manner, "What are you doing?" This snapped her out of her trance and we returned to our physical bodies.

I used to call moments like these "love at first sight." But now I know that it's just the Source recognizing itself in another. It feels *so* sexual—so much like love. But I know it's way beyond that. Having sex releases that built-up energy, but never completely satisfies the deep longing between two people. A *sustained* merging of light bodies is the only thing that would satisfy that longing. But that would require both people to be fully capable of such a feat.

But, in the meantime, I have experienced a most magical moment with another human being—true intimacy.

Saying Thank You

If she does something for you, no matter how small, say "thank you." If you part ways, be sure to thank her for the things she has helped you with, and especially for her patience as you fumbled with your own difficulties. Always strive with your partners to create something new, something beyond ordinary. Allow the love and the wish for her fulfillment to continue, for we all come from one Source. Never deny affection, and never cut her off in your fear. There is no need to do that anymore. Besides, you can never leave someone who is aware.

Friends

I see someone who recognizes who I am, someone who knows me and loves the real me where I have trouble loving and believing in myself. I see that she is aware of me in the most intimate and ultimate way. She sees past my walls, my fears, my little thoughts and failures. She sees my light body and what it wants to be—what it has come here to be—and she wants me to attain that. She knows herself—her light body—and what she wants for herself. She is my perfect partner, but even more, she is my best friend.

Saying You're Sorry

There was a time in my life when I firmly believed that apologizing meant that I had not been aware of what I was doing, that I had done something unconsciously, and so for many years I did not apologize to anyone. Eventually, I understood that an apology could simply be a way of saying that I felt saddened by the confusion and pain, and wanted to express my own sadness over the event.

"My heart told me to tell you that it was sad when you were sad, and it was afraid when you were afraid. And I just wanted you to know this because I love you, and it hurt to see you cry. I am so sorry."

Love

The word "love" sucks. It is so overused, and yet it's the only word that can express a deepness of affection that is so rarely and deeply felt.

When I stopped loving myself and others (when the reptiles taught me that emotion was indulgence and I bought it),
my body fell apart. I thought my deterioration was everything
except a lack of love. "I know, it's my food! No, wait, it must
be my defective body. Oh, I know, it's a lack of oxygen and
ozone. No, it's the fluoride in the water."

Many tried to love this cold-hearted version of a reptile,
but only one held on against the odds. And she is still here.
Finally, the love sank in and opened me back up. Now we can
go forward. Thank you for the patience and stubborn love of
people. There is an abundance of good nature everywhere.
Only when we look with the eyes of fear do we see otherwise.

We have been missing the marriage of Love and Power.
Not wishy-washy, namby-pamby love, I'm talking about love
coupled with FORCE. Believe me when I say that we as a people have *completely forgotten* about the magnitude of the *force*
of love when allowed to ignite all of the chakras and consume
us. This is not seen in our culture.

Vulnerability is power. What? Isn't vulnerability weakness,
opening yourself to outside forces? No! When you close yourself off, you restrict the flow of power. Get it? When you open
yourself, you can assimilate *any* power, including negative
power, once you have mastered yourself enough to be solid.

Love all, for they are all aspects of yourself and the
Source. All creation waits in anticipation for you to seize the
moment and spin them around, bathing them in the fairy tale,
the mystery—the romance of passion. We all want the unbridled passion of the fictionalized tale—why not make it real?
They're just waiting for you to do it.

My heart sees things that my eyes do not. I need my heart
to talk to my eyes. "What do you see? What is the magnificence that you perceive? A multidimensional love affair? Beautiful beyond belief."

Forever

Does love really ever die? Don't you still feel love for all of your old girlfriends—or at least most of them? Then what is it that keeps you apart? It is because your energetic paths have diverged. She went to a certain plateau in her journey through life, and then decided to stop in that cul-de-sac and explore only the things in that neighborhood. You have decided to keep going until you find the Source that pushes and pulls you constantly.

The secret to a lifelong relationship is having the pursuit of energetic self-fulfillment in common. If two people are constantly evolving—walking past fear within themselves and within their relationship—then they will always be together, even if their journeys take them along separate roads for a time. With a partner who seeks the ultimate, you will always find each other again and again. And you will bring with you a greater capacity for joy, courage, and vitality as you walk with your dearest friend into forever.

The Doll

The sun set a while ago and now the wind is picking up as I walk across a desolate plain. Everything is gray and damp since the rain earlier today. I am alone, but I like it.

There is someone standing facing me, not too far away. I approach her, but she seems stiff, almost lifeless. She wears a light, broken-in burlap robe with a large hood that hangs over her entire face, and she is rigid, with her arms folded across her chest and her feet shoulder-width apart. She reminds me of a Hopi kachina doll.

I stop just in front of her. I don't hear her breathing. My umbilical area is tingling and restless—thrilled. I sense something is already happening. I quickly reach out and throw back her hood. I am caught unawares by the inhuman cornhusk face with the sewn-up lips. But suddenly her stitched eyes unfold and her giant black swirling eye starts sucking me in, belly first. I like it, but fear the liberating void inside myself.

Then I am lying next to her and the water is rising around her.

"Don't you want to know?" she whispers.

"Yes, I do." I look at her face. But then as the eye pulls me down into my bowels, I wake up breathing heavily, throat dry and sore, limbs stiff and rigid.

4

Fear

If you live in fear, you draw all negativity to yourself, from people, animals, other energies, and bad experiences. Little fears are with you every minute of your life. It's these stupid little things that will eventually kill you. Pay attention to the little things.

Choose not to engage physically or psychically in events or thoughts that create fear. Do not contribute your energy in any way to that pool of fearful energy. Do not be one of the sheep—transcend! Choose at all times to disengage and not participate in anything that feeds darkness. Do not participate in conscious events, such as watching certain television shows, that reinforce or propagate fear. When people tune in together to a television show, they create a mass consciousness, with all involved contributing their energy to that negativity or darkness. The tendency of our society is to control us with fear. Choose spontaneity and passion. Hurrying is fear made physical—you are not in your body.

If you have a feeling that bad things are going to happen and you *promote* that feeling by spreading it to others and coloring it with your own addition of darkness, then the reality is that you *want* bad things to happen. You have added to that negative energy and encouraged others to do the same! Sometimes people get each other so wound up that they actually attract entities that can *assist them* in producing dark events.

You have the power to influence the outcome of *all* events. Even if your bad feeling is an accurate premonition, the final result of the event can still be altered. Work to alleviate or lessen the final result by utilizing your power and consciousness to influence others in a *positive* way. *See* in your own vision an opening. Open your heart so that better things happen, or so that great learning and awakening take place. Don't feed the bad with your own laziness and lack of courage; don't secretly wish for disaster because your own life sucks ass and you haven't done a goddamn thing about it.

Be the man behind the scenes, the magician who's aware of his part in this dream. Choose to create tranquility, harmony, friendship, companionship, peace, and richness—anything that feeds the creation of love. Influence others with your positivity, at a distance and in person.

When you love everything and have real peace inside, then everything loves you back, even the bogeyman. If a maleficent person looks into your eyes, what he sees is that you accept him as a piece of the Source—now this is *real* power. We are all looking for our home and our family; even crooks have someone they love. When you throw fear on everything, then it shits down your throat and everything turns sour within you.

When your mind is still, agitated people and animals have nothing to react to and they will see you as nonthreatening. They will also recognize something greater than themselves in your eyes.

The Illusion

Fear is *always* an illusion. Understand this: Fear is *never* real. It has been given to us by forces that feed off of fear. It is not ours! It is an illusion, a subterfuge, a bold-faced lie! If you have a fear of a food, the food will not necessarily hurt you, but the fear sure as hell will.

The point is not to fear or prejudge anything or anyone, at any time. You need to be fearless *at all times,* no matter what "premonition" or thought chokes you. That way you use your creative energy to manifest positivity even when surrounded by negativity. Go there, see it, and live it. Fuck convention, fuck conformity, fuck judgments and stigmas, fuck belief systems, and fuck your stupid thoughts! Stand squarely in any situation or before any person without the slightest trepidation or hint of flinching. *Get what you want—always!* Be entirely fearless.

If you are afraid of getting screwed, you will be. If you are afraid of going somewhere, then you will stay home. If you are afraid of being different, then you will always be the same old hack. If you are afraid of making waves, then you will drown in your stupid suffocating boredom. If you are afraid of speaking out, then you will never inspire anyone, including yourself. If you believe in victimization, then every time you interact with others you will get taken advantage of. If you are afraid of evil energies, then they will attack you, suck your life force, and leave you for dead. You will die from not living. You will die from retreating. You will die from turning your own energy in on itself instead of letting it fly. Life ends where fear begins.

Trust yourself implicitly and *absolutely.* Don't ever worry about failing or making mistakes. If somebody says that you failed or made a mistake, tell them to fuck off—at least you gave it a shot. And know that if you keep at it, you will perfect it, and the critics will be left sucking your big pie hole.

Say to your light body, "Whatever you want." Say it over and over until you manifest everything you desire. Never think about anything, never worry about anything, and don't pray! Why not? Because praying supposes a separation or distance between you and the Source, and there is none. Division between you and your light body is the reason for failure, fear, lack of confidence, and all confusion. Do not judge yourself or anyone else. Follow the light.

Fear equals negation equals bondage. Bondage equals boundaries equals binding force. Binding force equals imprisonment equals disorder. Fear in your body is the cessation of the flow at that place, or within a given chakra. It is *learned*. It is assimilated. It is not yours.

Being afraid *for* others is like injecting poison into their food. Why would you do that? I'm sure they have enough trouble conquering their own fear without you adding more of your own. You might as well stay at home, or get as far away from them as you can if you are truly their friend.

The Riddle

Now, understand this: The energy behind fear *is* the Source! That's why fear can be so powerful. The energy of the Source is supposed to flow through you and everyone else completely unhindered. It is supposed to manifest through you as unbridled power, spontaneity, and joy.

Your beliefs, however, behave like a funnel and take that huge, gargantuan torrent of pure energy and try to cram it through the narrow, restrictive, and supposedly protective channels that you have adopted for yourself in your fear. Then that energy bottlenecks and stagnates. This restriction is what you have learned to call "fear." It is a trick, a distortion of the Source. So instead of letting go, you panic and create more restrictive patterns to try to protect yourself further.

You just need to get that energy out, and it's all jammed up inside of you. This is where your plethora of fears comes from. This is why fear never ends. This is why if you focus on the fear itself, it splinters and multiplies. It is a division, or fragmenting, of your life-force energy. All this fear creates insensitivity.

The answer to the riddle is to see the total illusion of fear and your own resistance to flow! Now get the hell out of the way of yourself and watch what you can create. It will be messy, out of control, and thoroughly unpredictable. But, man, what a rush it will be. Things will appear out of the thin air—opportunities, people, events, more energy, joyful creations, creativity, money, health, spontaneous remission, love, affection, joy, laughter, peace, serenity. Can you imagine? Can you let go?

The only way to disengage fearful energy from your past is finally to face the energy of that past event without flinching or running away. Be afraid, and do it anyway.

Your light body will continue to bring greater challenges into your life until the moment that you chicken out. Your light body pauses when you run away in fear, but it holds the lesson right where you left it. It will not present you with greater challenges nor manifest greater gifts until you face that fear. So why be afraid? You've got nothing to lose but your fear.

Let it pass out of you, right through your base chakra and into the Earth. Let it dissolve. If you don't let it pass, it will get stuck in your base chakra and you will stain your pants.

Emotional Fear

It's relatively easy to understand physical fright, but much more difficult to understand emotional terror and the associated fears. Fear is often used as an excuse for avoidance of heavy emotion; you want to forget certain memories because they are too painful for you. What you are truly saying, though, is that you don't want to feel the depth of your love and openness. And so you use fear as a protective device. This is where the deep-seated challenges are encountered and real courage is born. Which is stronger, your fear or your love?

Letting go of fear, or getting over fear, does not mean that you suddenly become happy. Letting go of fear means that you let go of your fear of emotion—the tension or holding of your breath that separates you from the emotion and the flow of your life force. When you let go of your fear of emotion, then you can settle into the emotion that raised the fear.

There is fear of joy and happiness, fear of failure, fear of loss, fear of power, fear of anger, fear of love, fear of being in your body and using it to feel the world, fear of sexual or creative energy, and fear of evolution, which is really a fear of leaving your comfort zone. There is fear of losing what you know and freefalling into the powerful and uncontrollable depths, and fear of expressing your Truth.

When you label or judge your emotions as good or bad, fearful or not, you create a "tie-in" to what *others* believe about that emotion. This makes it harder for you to sort out the reality of what is going on inside *you*. Instead of judging your emotions, try letting go and just swimming around in the emotion to see how you feel about it. This is what letting go of fear is really all about—encountering your emotions head-on.

Just sit there quietly and let the emotion rise up. Don't think about it at all. Just feel. Feel how it tries to get you to feed it with bad thoughts, or thoughts of how you might be losing your sanity or getting a disease, or how you might want to hurt yourself. Don't freeze up. Don't clench. Relax every part of your body and *breathe*. Let the feeling move in your body. It will circulate and dissipate. Do this every time you feel choked by fear of emotion.

Think of an instance in your life when you were afraid of something. Maybe you were afraid of a certain food, like cauliflower, or maybe you were afraid of roller coasters or of tongue kissing. But once you let go of your fear and tried it, you couldn't even remember what the big freakin' deal was.

Some people unconsciously use emotional fear as an adrenaline high, a rush, a way of forcing themselves to relate to the world. They let it build up until they explode. Using fear in this way encourages movement, but in an antagonistic and hysterical way. It depletes your adrenals and ends in exhaustion. Love and self-awareness are much better ways to relate to yourself and the world. They produce an effortless path through life.

Evil

To label something as "evil" is to give it a superior or lofty status, a position above common everyday forces. Labeling something as evil elevates its power above your own, thereby giving it power over you. Now you have made yourself the victim. The word "evil" contains the power and the elevation. Otherwise, you would just refer to the person or event as troublesome, sad, or a nuisance—a lesser status, and a more easily controllable one.

Referring to a person or event as evil demonstrates just how much you fear or even are *impressed* by a particular force. It indicates that its source of power has an element of mystery to it, or that it is outside of everyone's control. It indicates a sense of awe and a potential to worship.

Evil is more accurately described as violence, and violence is extreme fear, repression, and hurt—hardly something to admire. But if you have your own fear, anger, and hurt crammed way down inside, well . . .

The only mystery here is why you have never faced the fear, anger, or hurt within you. Why do you remain boxed in a corner?

It's the people who refuse to acknowledge the reality of the world that are so shocked when that ugliness erupts in front of them. They are the perfect victims, the most ignorant of cowards, the most pathetic of fools. They are afraid of the darkness within them—the repressed and now soured emotions, and the force of their very beings that they have locked up. They are afraid of revealing themselves, and they are afraid of being revealed.

A man of darkness is too much of a wuss to face his emotional past, and so he elevates himself just enough to be able to inflict that same fear and hurt on others. He's too weak to fight his own battles or take responsibility for his own lack of self-worth, and so he relieves his pain through violence.

We, as a culture, have elevated certain events and people in this way. We instill fear and a sense of victimhood into our children. Why have we done this? What kind of courage can we expect from a child who believes in evil? How will this child ever grow into an adult capable of creating a world of magic if it sees that its parents and leaders believe in their own victimhood? Our media bombards us with this mind-set. It is pathetic.

Violence

A person who becomes violent because of society is our own nasty stepchild—a repugnant reflection of our degraded values and standards. Violence is a darkness that has never known the light, and desperately needs to see it. All creation comes from one Source, and all creation will return there. The power of darkness is limited—a very narrow and brittle power, a power that is incomplete. But no creature of darkness has to give up its power; it only has to enlarge it by walking past its fear and embracing the light. What a rush. What a fulfillment.

Darkness is a distortion of light energy—a fragment, an aberration, or a misalignment. It is a subset of the whole. If you believe otherwise, then you will find yourself believing that our universe is eternally divided into opposing sides, constantly at war, and never to be united.

White light contains all colors within it. Prisms refract white light into its various components. Your perception is a prism. Your beliefs are a prism. If anything other than white light comes out of you, then there is fragmentation within you, and you need to examine that.

It is imperative that you utilize your ability to perceive more and more of the components of light. By doing this around others, you assist in shattering their faulty perceptions. You do not get caught up in their aberrations. Everything is energy. Everything is from the Source. Whatever darkness there is must be rounded up and assimilated back into the whole.

Violence creates violence. If you want war to cease, then you must be rid of the anger, frustration, and hatred within you. Do you tailgate when you drive, trying to manipulate the person in front of you through fear? How are you any different from a government that uses fear to get what it wants? Does your company strive to squash its competition? That is violence. More fear equals more potential for violence. Do you badger and nag your spouse or partner? Why are you projecting your fear and frustration onto her? Violence and war are inside *you*.

Every time you buy into a collective fear, your energy goes into a pool that feeds those who are tuned to darkness. *You* are feeding *them*. You are using your *creative* energy to *create fear*. It is *your* undoing. Every time you watch or hear news of darkness and you feel a twinge of fear, you have fed that pool, and they grow in strength.

And if you run in fear from the darkness, you are still feeding the darkness! The only way out is to move through your own fear. This doesn't mean that you will not encounter darkness; it means that you *choose* to open your heart in the face of fear. You have discovered courage.

A man of power and light faces his own demons without fear of failure. By facing his fears, he expands his energy and his awareness, and swallows the darkness that terrorized him. He now knows that, because he has swallowed his darkness, he has reintegrated that energy in himself. He is now capable of facing that darkness in others.

As you raise your vibration, you become inaccessible to lower forms of energy, both physically and energetically. They won't be able to find you until they find that higher vibration in themselves. And when they do finally find that vibration, then they will have evolved into a friend; they will no longer be your enemy.

We have created this darkness. We must rectify it. And the way to do this is by understanding our own need for power. We deny ourselves power—our own birthright. The power to be absolutely extraordinary, to command our destiny, to manifest magnificence, to ooze brilliance and joy, to master the flame within us, and to astound ourselves and the world with our thoroughly virile force is our legacy. The power of fulfillment is happiness and light, and is always stronger and more magnificent than any evil.

Reptiles

Many years ago, a friend of mine made me aware of what he called *empties*. He saw that they were humans without souls. Another man I knew made references to *inorganic beings*—humans that had no light bodies. Around the same time, I had the most bizarre relationship with a woman who loved to keep me in the dark, twist everything I said, and run me ragged with sex, loss of seed, power struggles, and emotional upheaval. She seemed secretly to get off on it. My friend said she was an empty.

Eventually, I started to see that these empties all behaved the same way. They could twist any truth or lie to fit their task at hand, seem totally heartless without any guilt or remorse, use sex to render a man or woman worthless, create thoroughly engrossing and depleting dramas, and always be aloof and cold except when it was necessary to display a calculated affection. Some would describe them as being possessed.

Then I realized that some people were calling them reptiles. Reptiles are an ancient race with human bodies and the heads of serpents. The story of the serpent tempting Eve is based on the reptile that first seduced Eve. Regardless of what you call them, the fact is that reptiles create emotional turmoil and feed off it. I have seen it firsthand.

Reptiles inhabit the bodies of empties and, as public figures, incite fear, anger, and confusion in the masses. They wreak havoc and consume our emotional spikes as food. They appear to be human, but they have no light bodies. Some very sexual women are not human—literally. They are reptiles that intend to keep as many men as possible preoccupied with sex, lust, and ejaculation. They are very powerful and will give you the best sex of your life. And even when you are too tired for more, they will lure you in *just one more time.*

There are also reptiles who take over the bodies of young children that have been so traumatized by abuse, violence, or fear that their light bodies are driven out, leaving a practically empty vehicle. The reptile commandeers the body and uses it until the body ceases. A reptile, flyer, or similar fear-focused entity can also displace the light body of a cowardly person focused on the darkness. But they can *only* eject a light body if the person *allows* fear to rule.

The drama created by reptiles can never be rationalized or explained with any logic. It will always seem like they love you one minute and hate you the next. But you will be so completely intoxicated by their power that you will desire against anyone's better judgment to continue to ride the wild emotional roller coaster and allow them to control you. This is not about psychology; these are not emotional cripples. They are entities from a different time and place, and you can bet your bottom dollar that therapy has no effect on them whatsoever.

Reptiles also create, and then suppress, injustices on purpose so that the injustices can later be revealed, thereby creating more anger and outrage as "justice" is served. The end result is the same—energetic food. The only solution is to disengage completely from the entire drama.

Everything they do that appears compassionate, kind, or even absolutely insane is a complicated sleight of hand, designed to lure people in closer so that the next wave of pain will produce an even deeper reaction. The shock factor is what produces spikes of emotional energy that they consume. They can be your best friend, turn around and stab you in the back, then make up with you and lure you in a little deeper. The drama intensifies. They will gain control over your upper chakras by helping you to drain your lower ones. But things don't always go according to their plans. Sometimes people wake up.

I have lived and worked with reptiles. They are powerful and intelligent, but they all lack human warmth, a deep sense of humor about life or themselves, deep-seated emotion, and any sense of right or wrong. The only law they have is self-protection and to remain concealed in their human disguise at all costs. They always give the impression of being very well rehearsed in their characters, and you will almost never catch them off guard. But something in you will always sense their darkness and the absence of a light body. Sometimes their power may strike you directly in your solar plexus or second chakra. Reptiles use humans that they have conquered to destroy other humans and animals.

In my own state of ignorance, I once tried to get one of

them to face its fear. It recoiled very violently and I caught a glimpse of the blackness and searing anger at its core. It is immense and frighteningly profound.

The bottom line is that we all must evolve or get off the ride. So make your choice.

Turbulence

I was staring down from 35,000 feet at the Rocky Mountains, as our jet was taking a good beating from the late summer afternoon turbulence. The televisions were on, along with the seat belt lights, and everyone, including the captain, was more than a little bit rattled by the length and severity of this particular thrashing. The captain had already expressed his bewilderment over the fact that all of their equipment and weather personnel had predicted perfect flying conditions. He had even taken us up another 5,000 feet.

The view from my window seat was beautiful, as usual, and I was marveling at all of the unpopulated spaces below. I was consciously working on letting my fear go, over and over, as waves of it kept arising from many of the other passengers. Everything was locked down, and the stewardesses and stewards were all strapped in, too, ignoring the bells that kept going off as various people kept pushing the overhead panic buttons.

I was on my way back from a trade show where I had been promoting my first book. It had gone very well, but I could tell that something was still missing. People were looking for more—much more—and I really wanted to unlock that within me. Their resonance was my resonance; we weren't just looking for whitewash or platitudes. We were looking for something raw.

After releasing another wave of fear and pulling myself back into my body, I spoke inwardly to the Source about my intention to go as far as I needed to release that resonance—the buried keys. Once again my unrelenting desire to create a viable reality that would never interfere with this path surfaced. I silently invited the assistance necessary in moving forward without flinching.

Something beckoned me at that moment and I looked away from the window. Along the bottom of the silent televisions hanging in the front of the cabin was a blue banner that read, "How far do you want to go?" I laughed out loud.

"All the way," I said, as I turned back to the window, still chuckling.

5

Gold

One of the truly fascinating recent discoveries came about when David Hudson, an Arizona farmer, rediscovered the alchemist's dream. At the time, he was trying to recover gold and silver chemically from his soil, but kept finding an unknown element interfering in the mix. After investing many years and millions of personal dollars in research, he and some of the scientists involved realized that they had discovered—or better yet, *rediscovered*—the monatomic elements, also known as the white powder of gold.

According to alchemical and ancient texts, the white powder of gold is the manna, or food of the gods. The wisest and most magical of the ancient empires flourished because they knew how to turn gold and other platinum group metals into their monatomic or high-spin state. In this state, the metals cease to be the materials with which we are familiar, and instead become a white powder that looks something like powdered sugar. This transpires when 46 percent of the element is transformed into pure energy and the metal bonds are broken. In this alchemical process, the gold is opened and its hidden powers revealed. It is exalted and reborn.

The white powder feeds the *connection* between the light body and the physical body because it exists in both worlds and can be consumed. It assists in the merging of the two bodies so that they once again function as a whole. The white powder stimulates the endocrine system and, in conjunction with your desire to go beyond what you know, produces an internal biological evolution. Now your light body can fully communicate with and manifest in your physical body.

The Egyptians classified this as food for the light body. But there are also regular foods and herbs that contribute to this marriage as well, such as carrots, concord grapes, sheep sorrel, slippery elm bark, and aloe vera, since they are naturally high in the monatomic elements rhodium and iridium. For these foods to be optimal, however, they need to be farmed on rich volcanic soil.

These monatomic elements are the missing physical links in regard to intuitive and developmental states that used to be more abundant when our soils were not so depleted, and our water and air not so filthy and so taxing to our systems. We have the potential to go way beyond our current reality.

The onset of depression and fear in teenage years is a direct result of the loss of monatomic elements due to the onset of menstruation for girls and loss of seed for boys. This is the beginning of the breakdown of the connection between the light body and the physical body. This loss of contact with the Source is the loss of ability to manifest physically the power of Light. When my own physical body became depleted of monatomic elements, it absolutely came unglued. Without its solid connection to my light body, it lost its direction and was filled with anxiety around the clock.

With sufficient monatomic elements in your system, you just *know* things. You are plugged in. When the light body and physical body are reunited through monatomic elements, then no agent of destruction can affect the physical body because the light body is the most potent force in the universe. Coupled with your determination to make use of your latent abilities, you have the real ability to evolve. Then, after the monatomics have reawakened your dormant physical functions, you can continue the journey without the need to supplement them.

Healing and Monatomic Elements

The effects of monatomic ingestion are cumulative (see Resources and Suggested Reading for additional information). By rebuilding what should've been your body's natural supply of monatomic elements, you bridge the gap between the energy of your light body and its ability to manifest its power in your physical form. An energy worker who has increased his storehouse of monatomic elements will have the ability to effect lasting changes, perhaps even clearing the original chakra blockages in himself and others. But the healer *and* the healed must have the desire to become a vehicle for the Source and its manifestation. Otherwise, you will both just piss the monatomic elements right out.

Without sufficient monatomic elements, everything we do lacks transdimensional power. With the presence of monatomic elements in the system, the intention of the healer becomes physical as well as energetic, whether he's working on himself or someone else. The physical flows from the energetic.

The monatomic elements themselves do not eliminate the need for any therapeutic inner work, but instead supplement and enhance your abilities and create a tangible bridge between your light body and the physical world. They will produce a substantial urge to surround yourself with silence, and also enhance the regurgitation of your past. They can enhance the conscious dreaming state *only* if you are connected to the feeling-tones of your chakras.

We are supposed to be transdimensional beings. We were certainly born that way. But some children were raised in very depleted environs, and so they have no knowledge whatsoever of their vast potential. Practically all of the human race is deficient in monatomics.

Our practices, meditations, and will are nothing without the presence of monatomic elements. Lacking them is similar to a child waving a flashlight with dead batteries in a dark room—we are thoroughly robbed of our energy. Many things are practically impossible given our current state.

Your body knows when you are bent on unlocking its secrets and enhancing its abilities, and when it senses this, it absorbs more monatomic elements both from the powders and from food for direct intuition. A healthy endocrine system encourages a healthy body. Disease and its causes will endlessly multiply as we spiral further away from our optimal state.

Crystals and other stones resonate and amplify energy when it's of a strong enough frequency, but without monatomic elements the bridge between our will and the physical world is too weak to activate these stones sufficiently. The sympathetic vibration is too weak to be of any real healing use. When you have enough monatomic elements in your system, then stones work with you because you are able to connect with them.

The Kitchen

At the door to a kitchen tiled in pale green, a young but mature woman greets me. She has highly stylized eyes, almost Egyptian, but extremely vivid and intense. I perceive that she is tremendously aware and I recognize her from somewhere deep in my past, but not from this lifetime or even the one before. It was not even a love or sexual thing, but far deeper and broader. The feeling resembles something like, "I can't believe you're still alive—I was sure I would never see you again—never."

She takes me into the old cafeteria-styled kitchen. It has long sink counters stretched lengthwise down either side of the middle and around the perimeter, with deep stainless steel sinks on both sides of the middle island. Everything is clean, and I get the impression that none of it has been used in over 30 years. A formless feeling tells me that she and I, and some others, left here at some point in the remote past, and are now meeting here again in some kind of reunion.

There are eight other young women there, four on either side of the island, and all exceedingly beautiful. They are all in their late twenties, bathed in a heady aura of voluptuous sexuality and innocence. But their beauty goes far beyond their appearance, and I feel as though I have been intensely involved with each of them in many ways that I cannot describe at all. I am shocked and very deeply moved to see them all again, from so long ago and so very far away. They are more real than most people from my waking life and, at the same time, they are ethereal phantoms. They all look at me with a mixture of heartbreaking longing and horror.

I turn to the woman who first greeted me. She is touching my shoulder.

"Why are they so distraught?"

"The last time they saw you was in kindergarten. They thought you were gone for good. Though they secretly hoped they would see you again—somewhere— they had given up trying because it's been so long. They knew that you had gone far, far away."

The woman with deep brown eyes, in the front of the left group, tells me that after I left them there their teacher kept them in check by threatening to show them a picture of me and "my eyes." They were horrified of this picture and the visceral fear that it aroused in them. It was too inexplicable and otherworldly.

I am stunned at this, too, because I can't remember ever having taken a picture like that, and I can't remember ever having been in this kitchen. I have no idea what could be so frightening.

Then it feels as though each of them glides over and merges with me, reminding me of where I came from and where I should be. After this, they move over to the back door of the kitchen and step out of the dream.

6

Bamboozled

Sexuality is unrealized spirituality.

Sex is your lusty creative energy or godhood turned out-ward instead of inward; you spend your time looking for someone to spill it on instead of using it to fill yourself up. Sex has become so overrated because men and women have no idea how much more they could have than sex.

It's really about reaching for something more—something greater. Men have forgotten how to hold their power. It oozes out constantly, or is discharged repeatedly through ejaculation and drama. Once a man reduces his exposure to the constant bombardment of half-naked and suggestive women from mag-azines, newspapers, television, movies, the Internet, CD cov-ers, beaches, malls, swimming pools, his home, grocery stores, schools, and so on, and reconnects to the Source, his interest in sex dwindles dramatically. He suddenly remembers that he has better things to do than fill holes and make babies. His pri-orities are completely rearranged. He has *chosen* something else.

Now his resources can be used for his own fulfillment rather than the satisfaction of his and his partner's insecurities and superficial urges. Women, too, can elevate themselves from sexual baby-machines to vehicles of the Source. This is not the prudish abstinence of our falsely portrayed religious icons, but is rather a lusty fight for a headier reality; our dominant physical function of reproduction simply takes a backseat to our higher and further-reaching desire for evolution. Instead of reaching for the quick fix and quickly losing juice, we are simply storing it up *with patience* for the bigger adventure. It's just a choice.

Derailing the programming is the biggest challenge. Immediate gratification is just that—immediate. How do you get past that? Maybe you just need a few more orgasm hangovers, or pain in your perineum, or another bad relationship based mostly on lust. But perhaps you can take a moment to listen to that repressed little voice that keeps asking you each time you ejaculate, "Is this all there is, boss?"

Sex is sex. Don't confuse it with love; they're not the same thing, not even a little bit. Sex is pleasure, the love of physical form. The desire to "make love" to a woman is always sexual; it is not love. Love for another human being is much broader and calmer, and less sharp or intense. The love that replaces sex is self-love and multidimensional consciousness— you get a stiffy for the Source and for yourself.

Depth with another human being is found *after* you find it in yourself—period—end of story. *Then* you can mingle with each other as friends and partners in spiritual evolution. It is possible to utilize relationships to help you grow, but only if you keep your focus on your evolvement. All of the grief, fear, and hollow emptiness comes from trying to find fulfillment through sex and another human being. It will never happen!

Sex is simply an excuse for your missing relationship with the Source. You might choose to have sex later in life with another evolved human, but you won't need to if you return to your own strength and begin regrouping your multiconscious abilities. Then you will have nightly relationships and love without wasting yourself.

Comparing the male and female orgasm is ridiculous. The male orgasm is a release of the best of himself into a woman.

That's why a man wants to withdraw into himself afterward; he's regrouping. The equivalent release of the female is actually childbirth itself. This is when the female completes the releasing of the best of herself into the creation of a child and gives it up to the world. Now she thinks less about sex for a while, too.

Sperm

Do not ejaculate. Not only are you giving up elements that your body had to expend great effort to distill, but you are giving up your youth, the precious elements that you were born with. Once you've depleted your original resources, it is very, *very* difficult to get them back. You can easily deplete yourself within a few years, but it can take five or ten to replace them. Time is not on your side.

The best of yourself is gone, given to another or to your local water reclamation project. What did you expect? Losing your seed depletes your body of monatomic elements, among many other things. It may very well be that because our bodies are already depleted of minerals, vitamins, elements, enzymes, and monatomic substances (thanks to soil depletion and other problems) we physically cannot sustain much loss of seed. One orgasm sends the body scrambling to gather the best of itself for the next round of procreation, leaving little or nothing for your own evolution or health. Men from hundreds or thousands of years ago could afford to throw a little seed here and there.

The Focus

People who are hung up on sex and fear losing it—since it's one of their only pleasures—try really hard to make it spiritual. In my experience, elevating my energy disengages me from any purely sexual interest and leads to a very clear and light mind. All chakras are aroused, and the strength and fire are evenly distributed.

When you have sex with orgasm on the brain, then you

have singled out a part of yourself at the expense of the whole. Focusing on orgasm is primarily a single-chakra experience and this is how you wind up draining yourself—one chakra gets overused. Each experience of your life should involve *all* chakras. When you learn to do this, you will find that you are emotionally balanced, powerful, and complete.

All is balance. One is *imbalance*. An orgasm requires that energy be drawn from all chakras, coiled up and agitated within the second chakra, and then released primarily through that chakra. This is how you create another life! You wind your energy up into a tight little ball and you release it into an egg. Imagine if you could do the same thing with your energy and focus it through any of your other chakras, such as sending your light body out at will. Consider that.

Personally, I no longer like the feeling of having my energy aroused solely for orgasm. I prefer to have all of my chakras glowing and balanced. I find it much more satisfying—and relaxing. Masturbation, too, is focused on one chakra. Learn to be your sexuality, which means that when you feel horny, your feet are horny, too, and so is your heart.

If a sexual woman approaches, you can feel an almost immediate shift as your energy drops, but only if you are not yet thoroughly convinced that you want something more. If a sexual woman is around and I allow my sexual energy to circulate without clamping down on it, I've found that I get a little jolt in my second chakra and a rush through the rest. I have to lock the energy down purposefully in my second chakra to get aroused. And usually the only time I do that is when my fear of rejection or loss kicks in.

Sexuality and the Chakras

Shortly after I had succeeded in storing enough sexual energy that it reinforced my upper chakras, I began a very serious and unbelievable journey into conscious dreaming. I was thrilled beyond belief, and the power surged in my bones. But, alas, I still had a serious weakness: I had not yet seen the difference between pleasure through the senses and the deeper and more lasting enjoyment of self-fulfillment. I gave it all up for lots of sex and drama. Within six months, I had lost the fruits of almost four years of very intense inner work.

Sexual energy is life force or creative energy. It feels good coming, and it feels good going. Storing it produces a pressure in the body, something we're not used to. You feel highly sexual and highly aroused all the time—like you could burst. And so you're more than ready to do just that.

Your sexual energy will arouse you *any time* it moves in your body. This is where the phrase "lust for life" becomes apparent. This energy is orgasmic. Period. It can be used for pleasure or it can be used for the less immediate goal of self-elevation. Self-elevation requires the *conversion* of sexual energy from being directed into the senses to being cut loose into your other chakras.

All chakras are capable of hoarding or coveting energy. The base chakra can hoard it for physical development over spiritual development, or the heart can hoard it at the expense of power development. The throat can hoard it and talk too much while being afraid of losing its form of expression; all other forms of expression may already be repressed.

Most of us are just used to being in a *depleted* state. A man who ejaculates daily is actually living in a constant stupor, a numb or subpowerful state. That's why it is so difficult to store orgasmic energy. You have to increase your tolerance or acceptance of a perpetual orgasmic feeling as you store the energy. You learn to let it ride throughout your body, making you horny as fuck all the way down to your toenails.

Now, as this energy builds and builds, you will want very badly to release it. But don't. Continue to store it and circulate it, again and again. Don't resist—circulate. Releasing it during the storing of it is very powerful, and you will have an orgasm like you've never had. Then you'll want more and you will have to start all over again. Women will want a big piece of you and will smell it on you from miles away. But keep it to yourself and stay focused and relaxed in the midst of your growing pains.

Understand that the release of your life-force energy is what death *could* feel like if you died in all your glory, and not as some pathetic shriveled corpse in a hospital bed. This is the final bursting, the joyful metamorphosis from this life to the next. The experience of death is the ultimate orgasm if you are at your peak. It is the ultimate release of life-force energy. This is why people in many ancient cultures ran to their deaths with open arms. They knew that it was powerful, and they were thoroughly enticed by it.

Today, however, we go out like suckers, wasted and impotent. Each time you ejaculate, you are experiencing a smaller form of this metamorphosis. It is an uncontrolled release of your life force, a secret desire to be free of the physical. You desire to be unencumbered and no longer trapped in your physical form. You long to return to your original state.

When you ejaculate constantly, you are literally swooning toward death. The expulsion of that energy is your desire for transformation. Orgasm is a dribbling out of your power over time. Storing your energy allows for a *full-chakra* orgasm at the *time of your choosing*. This is spontaneous human combustion, a burning from within. We have utterly forgotten about this kind of power or ability to choose the time, place, and circumstances of our death. This full-chakra power is what activates full consciousness and the capacity to see all energy as it flows in and around us.

If the primary focus of your energy is on your third eye and crown, you cannot get an erection, nor can you maintain one. If you try to arouse yourself, your energy will resist moving down. When you finally succeed, the light around your head will suddenly grow dimmer.

Our instincts are correct—we're silently looking for the ultimate. It's just that we've forgotten how. Ejaculation is the poorest utilization of your potentially vast resources. You have to willfully refuse to allow your most powerful creative energy to trickle out for some half-assed and *temporary* pleasure. If you want the ultimate in life, you have to do the work! And you're going to sweat bullets on your way.

Orgasm and Monatomic Elements

Instead of looking for a "fill-in" while waiting for your next partner to come along, explore the long-forgotten practice of self-love. I'm not talking about giving yourself carpal tunnel. I'm talking about learning to allow your sexual energy to move within your body without release. Men are conditioned to keep their sex energy glued to their sex organ. That kind of pressure demands release. So don't even touch it. Look, but don't touch. Let that desire fill your body instead.

By allowing that energy to move freely up and down your body, you will discover that there is a richness of feeling associated with sexual energy that is not restricted to your whanger. Allowing the energy to move freely makes you feel sexual in a nonfocused way and is very satisfying. The energy moves up into the higher chakras and elevates and strengthens their functions. There is a tremendous love within yourself for yourself.

Men used to experience waves of orgasm without the loss of sperm and without physical manipulation when monatomics existed in abundance in the physical body. Your body and brain still crave the hormones and energy released during orgasm. And yet, because of our depleted state, ejaculation further drains the body of monatomic elements, *absolutely*.

The desire to have children is the desire to perpetuate yourself, to create immortality. The presence of monatomic elements in your system allows you to do this within yourself, thereby lessening your desire to procreate. Sex loses its draw when you have found something more alluring.

If men and women had sex with other beings in their dreams like they used to, then men and women would only get together when there was truly something special between them.

When You Choose to Have Sex

Everything is a choice, and it is better to embrace something than to avoid it out of fear. So if you choose to have sex, look and see if you have any hidden motivations or fears—before, during, and after the act. If you are truly in love with another, the love will continue long after the sex is gone. Then if the two of you later choose not to have sex, at least you've made that decision based on your own energetic discoveries, and not because some old fart told you not to.

I used to be very goal-oriented: Insert unit, have orgasm. Then I had a couple of partners who told me that I wasn't done until they got their cookies, too. Well that was fine for a while, but then I started to wonder why I was the one responsible for everybody's orgasm. If I can get myself off, why can't she? I'm not her damn babysitter. Love and orgasms are *not* the same thing.

Your orgasm is an individual affair, not shared. Women get a kind of blank look when a guy is just pounding away. They feel violated on a deep level, like they're just being used. In the back of their mind, they're wondering why they're doing this and what is so exciting about it. They're wondering where the intimacy and affection are. They look into your eyes and see a man who has retreated into his own little world while looking for the laser light show. The only women that like full-throttle banging are the ones who aren't looking for intimacy.

The minute you focus on orgasm, your entire energetic makeup shifts and what should be an intimate connection becomes a battle over pleasure. Who gets it first? Haven't you ever had your woman say to you, "I just want you inside of me for a minute"—nothing else? She is looking for intimacy, not pleasure. You *want* to have intercourse without losing your chakra connections and life force. So have sex and forget the orgasm. Learn to be more sensitive to the communion of souls.

Choosing a Sexual Partner

Too often, a partner is chosen based on an itch or

convenience instead of waiting for someone with a more suitable frequency to come along. Many women—like many men—are on the path of least resistance. And the path of least resistance is indulgence in pleasure and pregnancy. For a sexual mingling to enhance the energetic natures of both people, the woman must intend for it as well. Otherwise, her focus will assist you in slamming your energy back down into your second chakra.

Without realizing it, a woman assists in the demise of her man by desiring his ejaculation; her energy will try to pull the man's energy into herself. His ejaculation soothes her own insecurities over whether or not she is irresistible and pleasurable. His loss of control makes her feel more powerful.

Intercourse allows for deep energetic mingling, so make sure you really like your partner. You are going to get the good and the bad all over you when you lock your vibrations with hers. You will experience her fears and she will experience yours.

During sex, a pathway is established between the two of you. Afterward, that pathway remains operative. Energy—good or bad—is transferred between the two of you for years, depending on the strength of the bond you created.

The Act

You and your partner undress. Stand about a foot apart and gently hold each other's arms just above the elbows. Just stand there for a few minutes. You already know you're about to have sex, so you don't need to rush. Just linger in the moment of anticipation and allow your energy to circulate in your body. Feel the rush, the excitement of anticipation. Then slowly bring her closer and feel the energy coursing between the two of you. Look. Caress. Kiss.

Eventually, you sit down with your legs crossed, and have her sit in your lap with her legs wrapped around you. Both partners are on equal ground. Your chakras are aligned with your partner's. Return to the feeling of love—the full heart rush. Remember, you can't have an orgasm unless your energy is held down in your second chakra—clamped, locked, and loaded. If your energy flows freely throughout your body, then your heart remains happy, you smell her rich skin, you look deeply into her eyes with full consciousness, you smile because your third eye is still open, and you laugh because your heart is energized.

Breathe. You feel connected to her, to yourself, and to the Source because your crown energy has not been sapped to fuel your orgasm. This kind of sex is like a lingering kiss, slow and deep. There is no overbalance in any one area and the heart leads the way. Here is where you can both make the world stop.

A heightening of the connection can occur if your reproductive glands—your testicles—touch the woman. The two small pouches for your testicles are just to the sides and above the base of the shaft of your penis. Your testicles can be gently maneuvered into their pockets where they will stay during arousal. If this is performed correctly, you will look as though you have labia surrounding the base of your penis.

If you have a woman sit on your lap with her legs wrapped around your lower back and you enter her, you will notice that her labia and your "labia" mate. Now the normally forgotten physical aspect of your second chakra (your testicles) is in physical contact with the woman. It is easier to control orgasms in this position.

You will find that after sitting inside of her for a while that there's a very quiet and *highly ignored* feeling of satisfaction and completion. Your body says that you can choose to withdraw now, *without orgasm*. Hold each other for a while, and then get dressed.

Your body will be very confused by this at first because you will still feel fully charged and aroused, instead of drugged and sleepy like you usually do after sex and an orgasm. Your urge will be to plunge back in and explode as you've always done. But don't do it! Play with this new peaceful, yet energized, satisfaction for a while and see what it brings up. It's possible that you will feel depressed after your arousal wanes because you didn't get your toy. But now you can see how you are attached to the goal, to the pleasure. You are really not interested in love and communion.

The Kama Sutra shows some other positions. These are not positions that you get into and then bang away. You strike the pose, hold it, and allow the energy to circulate. They are more like yoga positions that allow for the improved circulation of energy through different chakras and meridians. Each position has a different energetic influence.

This type of intercourse will move the female's light body out and intensify her dreaming. She may spend the rest of the day feeling very spacey because of this, so take care that she understands this and can function if she's going out. Her energy, however, will actually pull you further *into* your body. You may suddenly find yourself surrounded by a rich world that you forgot existed.

A Conclusion

There was a time in my teenage years when I only wanted to sleep with women with my clothes on. My light body was trying to tell me that sex was not the answer.

So what do you *do* with a woman who you don't have sex with? You share silence. You sit in a silent room and you each go deep into yourself. You both feel safe doing it because you know you won't interrupt each other. You can merge your light bodies while awake or asleep, recapitulate together, or hand-prepare food together. Now you share something thoroughly intangible. But guess what? That's what love and power are.

Boys

Some young boys were riding their bicycles outside my apartment one day, playing follow the leader and chasing each other. The youngest boy tagged along behind and watched them ride their bikes down a set of three concrete stairs. After the older boys had gone around the corner, he positioned his bike at the top of the stairs and felt the way that the older boys had done it. I was quietly watching him from my upstairs window, and I'll be danged if I didn't see and feel in my lower chakras a stabilizing current of energy proceed from the boy to the bottom of the stairs. Before he even started down, we both knew he had it.

But, just as he leaned forward to go for it, one of the older boys came riding around the corner looking for him and yelled at him to hurry up. There was a certain expectation and energetic command emitting from the older boy, who was saying with his energy, "You must maintain your level of inferiority and need around me—you must remain dependent on me. You are not old enough for this endeavor yet."

I watched as the younger boy retracted his current of energy, yet proceeded down the stairs anyway. All three of us knew he was done for. He bit it instantly, and fell in a tangled heap on his bike, crying. The older boy sighed heavily, and went to pick him up—all on cue.

7

Balance

The internal journey is much, much more difficult than any external journey, which is why so few have mastered the control of the light body or any of its powers. You are learning control over the nebulous, mastery of the intangible. Realizing the power of your chakras and light body is extremely esoteric stuff.

You have a north pole and a south pole. I first learned of the north and south poles while reading *The Emerald Tablets of Thoth-the-Atlantean,* by Dr. Doreal. If you exist in our current whacked-out society, then you have an overbalanced north pole. Our society's tendency to focus on the north pole is another reason for the deterioration of our health and our culture—we are out of balance.

Balancing the poles is about creating a *neutral* state in your physical form, a state that's neither positive nor negative. It's also a process of strengthening and enlarging each pole in order to create a more powerful neutral state. There is a hidden force behind your seeming neutrality, a silent but enormous current that is the void created when two powerful but opposing forces combine, producing a vacuum in time. You are this nothingness, and yet you are everything. Your light body also exists in this neutral state. Their perfect marriage can only occur if they vibrate in unison, resonate together in the void.

You will experience a lot of resistance to balancing your

poles: "I don't have enough time; I fall asleep every time I try it; it's boring; I don't really feel anything, anyway." You will also have to overcome your fidgety restlessness and your squirrelly lack of focus. The excuses are many for not doing it.

An overbalanced north pole can lead to diseases of stagnation: rumbling indigestion, headaches and migraines, insomnia or funky dreams, restricted lower chakras, and problems with your ankles, sexual organs, fingers, and nails. You will have trouble with cold feet and hands due to a lack of circulation. North pole strength is crucial in its activation of the upper functions of the chakras.

An overbalanced south pole can lead to diseases of indulgence: weight problems; flaccid body parts; laziness; lack of clarity; plugged upper chakras; atrophied thymus, hypothalamus, pineal, or pituitary glands; or a lack of communion with your light body and the Source. South pole strength is crucial for activating and circulating the feeling-tones of the chakras.

Be sure that your heart chakra is open and flowing when balancing the north pole and when balancing the south pole. The heart is the connecting link between the two poles, and its energy must mix thoroughly with each and its corresponding chakras. Become whole in each pole.

The Procedure

Balancing the poles takes two hours and needs to be done once per week if you show signs of imbalance. Lie flat on your back on a mat, with your head pointed north and your arms at your sides. Focus your energy from your heart through your head for one hour. If you feel one of your lower chakras igniting, gently pull the energy back up. Your eyes can be open or closed. Keep your body relaxed, and don't engage any thoughts.

We hold on desperately to our idea of self. This is physically a clenching in the center of your head. Shake it loose. Release the tension and flood it with energy and blood. Work on vibrating this center. If you've ever passed out, you are familiar with this vibration. It occurs just after the rushing in the ears and just before the actual loss of consciousness.

Focus lightly on your heart, throat, third eye, and crown chakras. Diverge your eyes and stare without focusing into space. Feel the throbbing in your head when your temporal lobes vibrate slowly in unison, and when the front and back of your brain do the same.

After one hour, swing your body around so that your head is now pointed south. Lower your energy so that it is focused from your heart through your feet. Do not allow your mind to engage at all since this will shift your energy back to the north pole. You can keep your eyes open or closed, and light napping is alright since it indicates that your mind is still. Actually, it is desirable to enter and hold that state just before sleep.

Try creating heat in the bottoms of your feet. Focus lightly on your heart, solar plexus, sexual, and base chakras.

While in both positions, notice how different thoughts or feelings pull or push your energy around or try to get your attention. Consider the items in the chart at the end of this section, and see how they relate to each pole. Are you primarily a north or south pole person? Which pole is easier for you to maintain a focus on? Which pole needs strengthening?

Balanced poles help to put you in a perpetual meditative state, an unforced silence. If your south pole is flowing properly, you will notice that when fear enters your body, it is immediately discharged through your legs and into the ground.

The vast majority of people alive are overbalanced in their north pole, which is why so many seek the south pole experiences—snorkeling in Hawaii, for example. But even when they get there, they don't allow themselves to let go and become fully immersed; they still cling to their north pole way of life.

Focus on what you need in order to attain balance instead of focusing on eradicating what you don't need. There is more strength and happiness in the positive approach. If you are balanced, then by the end of your day, you should still feel relaxed and connected. A pleasant heaviness will bring you to your bed.

North Pole Attributes (positive and negative)	South Pole Attributes (positive and negative)
Light body	Physical body
Spirit	Earth
Classical music	"Old school" funk music
Shallow breathing	Deep breathing
Head, shoulders, tops of joints	Fingertips, palms, legs, ankles, feet, and toes
Vegetarianism, veganism	Sensual, full-fat aromatic food
Mountains	Beaches
Talking, reading, writing, goal-driven focus	Touching, listening
Thinking, superficiality	Feeling-tones, emotions
Sexuality, fucking	Sensuality, energetic mingling
Fear, worry, anxiety	Love, affection
Universe	Bare feet, soles of feet
Studying	Meditation, sleeping, slumbering
Regurgitative dreaming	Conscious, lucid, or vivid dreaming
Frenetic activity, hurrying	Puttering
Showering	Bathing, soaking
Upper chakra functions	Lower chakra functions
War, conflict, fragmentation	Unity, wholeness
Security	Nakedness
Intensity, focus	Calmness, mellow wandering
Head, brain, eyes	Stomach, intestines
Running	Walking, meandering
Imagining, typing	Cooking
Mental exercise (aerobics, weight lifting, muscle toning)	Full-body development (yoga, Pilates, deep stretching and breathing)
Indigestion	Digestion, happy belly
Free radicals, toxins, "dead" foods, lack of oxygen	Raw foods, fermented foods, oxygen, enzymes

Fasting	Eating
Information, knowledge, facts	Intuition, gut feelings, wisdom
Power over others and things	Power combined with love
Time	Timelessness
Pointed vision or listening	Emotional smell, sound, touch, gazing
Problem-solving	Creating
Nightmares	Slumber
Leanness, scrawniness	Full-bodied form, obesity
Attentiveness	Laziness
Protection	Trust, openness

This list is in no way complete. You can see that there are positive and negative aspects of each pole. The manner in which an aspect is used can also reverse its polarity. For example, reading a book is typically a north pole function of the eyes. However, staring blankly into space is a south pole function of the eyes; your eyes absorb energy into your chakra system without linear direction.

Many of the south pole functions can be easily abused, leading to a pleasant forgetting of the inner work that needs to be done.

Nancy

Sometimes the way that things happen is just too perfect, like it was scripted and then acted out right in front of your face, just for you. It makes our belief in "coincidences" seem very flimsy.

At a clerking job I once had, an older customer, whom I'll call Nancy, found out that I had written a book. So she went to the local library and checked out a copy. I was just a tad nervous about her reading my book because I knew that there were some revealing things in it that many older people didn't like at all. I had already experienced the suddenly cold laughter and anxious politeness of many older and conservative coworkers who were shocked by the book's blatancy. So I figured Nancy and I would soon become ultra-polite and tense acquaintances.

I liked Nancy. She was a solitary transplant from the Midwest, satiric, intelligent, and outspoken. She didn't take any crap, had a great sense of humor, and was very alert. She was always alone. She came in and told me she was busy reading my book and didn't want to say anything until she was finished. Then she'd look at me out of the corner of her eye, shake her head with half a smirk, and walk out.

This went on for weeks. She'd even tell my coworkers to tell me "Nancy says hi" and "She's almost done." Finally, one day I was alone in the back room doing some work when she just walked in and plopped herself down in a chair facing me. She shook her head over and over, just smiling and laughing at me.

"You know yer certifiable, don't you?" She laughed. "Absolutely looo—neee."

I laughed, too, enjoying the way she dragged out "loony," despite her awkwardness. I fidgeted with a pencil.

"Why are you still in Oregon?" she asked point-blank.

"It's nice here," I replied. "I like the rain."

She stared at me, bewildered. "You don't belong here."

I nodded and laughed, knowing that she meant it as an irrefutable fact.

"Where're you from?" she urged.

"California."

She rolled her eyes. "Figures."

We both cackled.

"Don't you miss the sun?"

I nodded, as she looked knowingly at me.

"How can you do these mundane, boring jobs after writing something like that? I'd go crazy."

"They're only temporary."

She was quiet for a minute.

"Do you think all people have this within them, this power?" She wondered out loud, her index finger pressing her top lip.

"They do," I replied. "When I look into other people's eyes, I see a spark, a glimmer, a hope. It's like there's something always searching, looking for something more. They're just not sure where or what it is."

She nodded slowly. I could see she was immersed in her own thoughts. She looked first at me, and then off into the distance.

"I liked what you said about time and déjà vu's. Since I moved out here by myself, I've noticed that time has slowed down, gotten broader. It seems to expand as my attachments and interests fade. My kids are all grown up. I've tried just about everything."

"Mm-hmm," I agreed. "Our attachments are what anchor our perception to the cycle of time. Otherwise it loses its grip and things start to seem less real and much more pliable."

She nodded as she thought about it some more. "I'm not as concerned about things as I used to be. I used to think a lot about death—at my age . . ."

We both sniggered and shifted in our seats.

". . . and then I realized that I wasn't living. So I started living more."

When she said that, it caught me deep inside, like things always do when they register as Truth. I knew she was speaking for me.

"What have you got to lose by taking chances?" I rallied back, thinking of myself, too. "You can use this to spur you forward."

She raised her eyebrows and looked far away, and then fidgeted some more like she was ready to leave. I was kind of hoping she wouldn't.

"People don't like things or people that are too different, ya know," she announced as she stood up, winking at me and giving me a mothering glance.

"I know. But sometimes it just needs to be said."

"You gonna write some more?"

"I've got a few notes at home."

She rolled her eyes. "What more could you possibly say?"

Our mutual amusement finally caught the curiosity of some other coworkers. She headed for the door.

"Well, whatever you do, good luck," she insisted.

I saw her one more time after that. We exchanged knowing "hellos," and then I moved back to California.

8

Diseases of the Mind

Don't get screwed by your beliefs.

Back when I was in college, long before I had any inkling of light bodies or other energies, I took a course in classical philosophy. I was sitting in the second row, listening intently to one of my favorite professors rambling on about a particular philosopher that instructed his students to question everything, when someone behind me said, "Language is the downfall of mankind." I turned and glanced over my shoulder, but there was no one there.

This odd occurrence stuck in my mind for many years. Now, when I reflect back on it, I get an impression of two different utterances: the one I wrote down, and the one that my body remembers. The one that my body remembers is *"Thinking* is the downfall of mankind."

When I look around, I see the darkness of people, not dark as in evil or bad but dark as in heavy, attached, or weighed down by the beliefs that snuff out the inner mystery. They are surrounded by dark rooms that they have never explored, hallways lined with closed and locked doors, as my friend Court says. These restrictions are all self-imposed, and all it takes is a little effort, courage, and curiosity to open the doors and move beyond the constricting beliefs. Don't be afraid to let go of what you know.

Distorted perception, energetic blocks, faulty beliefs, bad genes, religion, science, patterns of the mind, words, symbols, crises, fate, and disease are all related—they are all static structures or interferences made up of energy. They are patterns that limit your flow of energy, and are arbitrary. If you become a "member" of one of these structures and utilize its systems and syntaxes, then you are bound energetically—consciously and unconsciously. Then you are kept very busy servicing your particular fragmentation of consciousness.

The choice to tie yourself to a structure can give you a sense of security or stability. But that stability has its price. The decision to disconnect from a structure disengages your energy and sets you adrift in a sea of possibilities without form. It is not easy to make sense out of the immensity of an ocean on a dark, moonless night if you are floating without a boat or life jacket. Structures and beliefs are boats, life jackets, flashlights, paddles, outboard motors, and two-way radios. The decision to go it alone and create your own system requires tremendous courage and a grand sense of adventure.

And yet this is freedom. Here is where your light body can create and modify its relationship to energy as it sees fit without having the added burden of other peoples' fears and negative beliefs: "Oh my God! Whaddayamean you don't have insurance? What if you get sick? What if you get c-a-n-c-e-r?" Or "Well, it's your choice if you leave our religion, and that's okay. I'd just hate to see you burn in hell, that's all." Or "That's just the way the system works. You're better off buying into it. Accidents happen, ya know!"

Yuck. Do you see how the fear traps people? They say you have a choice, but if you go ahead and bow out, they heap their own fear onto you. They know that if you succeed, then that shows that they have bought into a false paradigm. But if they can make you fail by heaping their own fear onto you, then you will return to the fold and be forgiven, and there will be no more reminders of life outside the box. Then everyone can be safe in their little prisons.

If you can't figure something out with your mind, it's because you haven't been there before. It is a totally unique place or state of being. Don't waste your time trying to impose a structure on something or someone that resists. Instead, give yourself to the originality and discover a new part of yourself, and a new way of life. When you give your energy free rein, then it can dream up answers that never existed before; this is creativity at its best.

Comparing your beliefs with somebody else's beliefs is *still* engaging in beliefs. Intuition never involves belief; there is only a bodily knowing. Energy flows when there is no impediment. *All* beliefs—good and bad—are impediments. Let's take a look at some of these scams.

Fate and Bad Genes

Fate and bad genes don't exist.

When things go badly for you, it's not some grandiose magnanimous deity testing you. It's not God challenging you. Everyone and everything on this planet has free will and anything goes. Other energies are free to act up and make waves to try to get a rise out of you. They are free to be unaware. You are free to walk away. If you do nothing, then nothing will change.

We test *ourselves;* these are our challenges and lessons. If things continue to go badly for you, then you are not listening to your light body.

Nothing "runs in the family." The *tendency* of family members to "inherit" similar conditions is based on a lack of energetic awareness, not on defective genes. You take your energy and create the physical scenario so you can live out the lesson. That's how much power you have.

The choice to be born into certain families with certain energetic blockages is an opportunity to *undo* that programming. You chose to accept the challenge to see beyond that collective familial fear (or its opposite) and smash it to pieces. Our peers and elders contribute to this psychic soup with their various fears and shortcomings, faulty perceptions, "past lives," or other issues.

Religion and Science

The core of any philosophy, religion, or syntax is its ability to alter perception in order to see energy from a new perspective. But why go from one religion to another? Why not just dump religion altogether? Get rid of the baggage forever.

Rituals and ceremonies are ways of trapping the attention and tricking the mind into being still and unaffected by anything from the outside. Combine a dim, candlelit room or outdoor scene with some solemn artwork, a little incense, drumming, dancing, chanting, liturgy, formal prayer, maybe a drug or two, and the intense energetic focus of a group of people and you've got a trance state secured from any outside influence. Now you can safely explore the energetic creation of this particular group. You are told you can believe in this, but not in that. It's all nice and neat, except for the fact that the parameters are arbitrary and based on somebody else's fear. Why not create your own parameters so that you are free to change them as you grow out of fear? Religions separate people. And religions separate people from themselves.

Modern science, too, is fragmentation, not unity. Things have been broken down too far, separated too much. Science's vision is myopic. It's time to become aware again of the whole, the bigger picture, and to focus on how to utilize what we have for our benefit instead of our destruction. The greatest science is within you, and is accessed and actualized when your consciousness encompasses the totality of you—your subconscious and unconscious.

What If?

What if this happens? What if that happens? Well, if she does this, then I'll do that. And if my boss says this, then I'll say that.

There is no "what if?" It is an absolutely ludicrous waste

of energy to engage in suppositions. Your fear is strangling you, trying to mangle the spontaneous nature of your light body. You can never prepare yourself for the inevitable. The only reality is "what I desire" in every moment of life.

Words

Words are deceptive. They funnel our thoughts into little pigeonholes. But all words have abnormalities or deviations. What one person means by a particular word may have a different coloration for another, and screw up the whole conversation.

Words are approximations of energy. Words are symbols of the intangible. Arguing over words or terms is an utter waste of time. See past the symbol and into the actuality, the feeling behind the words. Use your chakras, not your brain, goddammit!

Conversation is a metaphor for feeling. Look into the eyes. Listen to the intensity. Observe the body language. Read between the lines.

Duality exists because of physicality. The brain perceives paradox because the language can't wrap its linear or two-dimensional arms around *all* the dimensions of feeling. So the syntax of our language reflects opposites. That's why poets who seek to transcend duality will often use pairs of opposites to describe a *single* feeling or mood. They're trying to tell you it's somewhere in between—just beyond or above, or both. They seek to touch for a moment a completeness beyond opposites—the completeness of their own light bodies. Trying to describe the world of the Source makes it sound like a world of opposites, a world of paradox.

Words are tools. You follow your feelings and then you select the appropriate words to penetrate a person's obstruction and help that person to see more. To write those words down and call them dogma is to take the individuality out of each situation and injure the very people you are trying to help with your tools. Forget what was said in the past. What needs to be said now?

Words are never the actual experience—how can they be? Names and labels are restrictive. To use a label on a person is to segregate that person from the whole. You have isolated them with your belief expressed by your choice of words. They are no longer one with you. They are one step removed. It is irresponsible to hold onto labels or beliefs so tightly that they alienate other human beings. This is bigotry.

To choose not to label or classify an experience is to allow it to exist on many levels. To classify it is to restrict it to only a few levels. Fear is what constricts and limits.

Be careful of words that you give yourself up to, words that are allowed to exercise control over you. The word "addiction" is a perfect example. "It's an addiction of mine," you say. This implies that you have no control in the situation. Your choice of that word indicates that you are still giving your power to your addiction. Otherwise, you would never speak of it as being above you.

Patterns of the Mind

Anything that creates a pattern, such as talking, music, reading, or all of our electronics, locks the energy of the brain into a series of patterns. Instead of remaining multivibrational, as it does in stillness, it becomes narrowly tuned, selective, and restrictive. This effectively causes us to tune out vibrations or informational signals from other dimensions or people.

People who are highly receptive to multivibrational wavelengths and who are worried about *other people's* ideas of what is and is not sane will subconsciously surround themselves with constant distractions, especially at night, in order to be oblivious to what would otherwise be a cacophony of information received from within them. Perhaps as children they opened their mouths about other dimensions or energies, much to the embarrassment or fear of their parents, were immediately shamed and punished, and since then have never allowed those wavelengths to surface again.

When you make life choices based on logic, it all looks

great on paper, but it feels like shit. This is the key: Be absolutely free, not just free from others and from attachments, but free in yourself, in your own mind. Once you finally pierce the energetic bubble that holds you back, others will follow. But until someone finally pierces that energetic bubble, everyone is stuck.

In college, I had a gay friend, Dudley. Dudley called me one night.

"Matt, I've got a problem."

"What is it?" I queried.

"Well, there's this girl at work. I like her, and she likes me."

Silence on my end. "Uh, so what's the problem?"

"I *can't* go out with her," he stammered.

"Why not?"

"Cuz I'm gay."

I just sat there, baffled. Finally, I said, "If you like her and she likes you, then just go out with her."

"Oh, yeah," he said. More pausing, more thinking—"I guess I could."

Dudley had told himself, his friends, and his family so many times that he was gay that he couldn't see past his own patterns to see the answer. *All* beliefs are like this.

Changing the preprogrammed patterns of the mind injected by society involves chipping away at them, day by day, moment by moment. As you do, you save precious bits of energy, saving them up like pennies in a jar. The accumulation is barely noticeable, until the day that you notice the jar is full and you are able to unleash larger amounts of energy to fuel your intentions.

If you were fully conscious of the energy engaged in your current patterns of consciousness, you would be able to redirect that abundant energy at will. But this energy is hidden from you, locked up in a collective dream that you and others have agreed to create and play out. The effort to disengage from your clutching must be done deliberately and with constant attention—you are in the process of waking up.

Choice

When you live according to your fear, your world shrinks. There is less and less magic, and more and more drudgery. But when you begin to move beyond fear, then suddenly there is power and momentum. Your possibilities start to become realities, and everyone says you are blessed. But what has really happened? You have simply made a choice born of your awareness.

You decided not to be pushed down by fear. You decided not to be subhuman. Nothing was given to you on a silver platter. Nobody came to your home and handed you a million dollars. You busted your ass to rise above and achieve. This is a choice, and now you see that it has always been so. You do what you want.

When you came home from a shitty day at work and you were burnt out and tired, you didn't flop your lazy ass down in front of the television and eat microwaved trash. You came home and went walking in the hills, and then hand-prepared your own food with your own driven intention. This fed you more than any already prepared food you could've bought. And little by little, your strength increased and you knew it, and this further fueled your fire. And finally, you started to rise above your difficulties; your stupid job no longer had the upper hand. You became stronger than it.

You became stronger than the darkness that was always creeping along behind you, healthier than the toxins trapped in the building's germ-infested closed-air system, and more resilient than the hideous chattering of the hysterical people clamoring for distraction. You asserted your right to choose and create.

Compassion

Modern compassion is crap. "Oh, boohoo, you poor victim. Let me, who is greater and better than you, help you to be more like me—the magnanimous and pompous wise one. You poor baby, you are so wretched in your lack of awareness and need to grovel in poverty and self-pity that I instantly run to your aid and save you from yourself! Look at me, everyone. See my compassion on display. I am the savior of those who *won't* save themselves."

This compassion is another veiled form of arrogance. It is a belief that others are inferior to you. If you don't have confidence in them, then you don't have confidence in yourself. If you pick them up, it is because you fear that you will need to be picked up one day. The victim has a need to be taken care of, and the savior has a need to be depended on and admired.

But this doesn't mean that you don't work together. It means that you don't cater to those who won't pull themselves up so that you feel worthwhile. Be strong together. That is what partnership is.

Your Magnificent Brain

Science declares that only a small percentage of your brain is being used because its higher function has not been fully realized. The entire brain is a chakra; it is the crown of higher emotion and feeling.

We have been taught only to use the brain for its lower function, its rational and logical thinking processes. But this is like using your index finger only for scratching your cracks. Your brain is dynamic and creates physical pathways within itself according to your environment and your emotional relationship to it—energy becomes reality.

Your chakras are supposed to send an absolute wealth of information directly to your brain to code your reality. All kinds of intimations, impressions of energy, feelings, colors, moods, vibrations, memories, signals from other people, frequencies from the Earth or animals, weather fluctuations, intuitions, "psychic" details, and densities or signals too weak to be picked up by your five senses should be as common as the smell of meat-balls in an Italian restaurant. This should be your reality. Then your entire brain would be engaged. But instead, you're left with the dregs of existence, your subhuman condition.

The most fascinating thing about the brain is that when it is functioning in its *lowest* capacity as a rational tool and chatterbox, it is cycling at its *highest* frequency. If it remains at this high frequency for too long, it stresses out your body. When your brain slows down and cycles at lower frequencies, however, the rational tools are turned off and it becomes aware of the bigger picture. It has major revelations and seeks to change destructive behaviors. As it approaches its slowest rates, it cycles at the same frequency as the Earth and its creatures, heals the body, and becomes timeless and meditative.

Cell Fermentation

Without sufficient monatomic elements in your system, your light body cannot properly merge with your physical body. When the flow of light decreases, oxygen levels diminish and heat builds up in your system. For your cells to stay alive, they resort to cell fermentation, a more primal form of survival based on the conversion of glucose to energy, rather than their preferred method of converting oxygen to energy.

Cell fermentation is cancer, and it occurs because of a lack of oxygen and light at the cellular level. Tumors ferment sugar. Good cells burn oxygen. If you think too much over an extended period or have an overbalanced north pole, your cortex becomes inflamed, suffocating and starving the innermost portions of your brain. These innermost portions are your emotional and instinctual brains, and your direct link to your lower chakras.

This lack of oxygen in the brain and body creates an anaerobic environment, which is the preferred environment of bacteria and parasites at some stage of their evolvement. An anaerobic environment allows "bad" bacteria and parasites to proliferate, thereby damaging and taking over various bodily organs, and filling your cells and organs with toxic wastes.

Cell fermentation is always systemic, meaning that it does not show up in only one place, but pervades your entire body. If you have a particularly weak or distressed organ or body part, you will experience a localized condition: a lump, abnormal cell growth, discoloration, rash, cancer, and so on. Cancer usually only occurs after decades of chronic cell fermentation. Because your entire system is suffering and your body is trying desperately but unsuccessfully to mop up the diseased cells, your adrenals and lymphatic system will also be fatigued. When a particular lymph node is overrun with diseased cells, it does not mean that the node is cancerous! It means that it is doing its job, but is unable to keep up with the chronic production of diseased cells.

Once cell fermentation sets in, anything can exacerbate it. If you have a fairly mild condition and you experience its effects as rashes, then a food can seemingly be an allergen when maybe it is only aggravating the condition. Stress from work, too much talking, reading too fast, too much drama or sex, or not enough sleep will do the same.

Cancer

Cancer is like herpes—we all have it already. We all have cancer cells and we all have herpes cells. But we don't technically "have" a disease until a certain threshold is crossed. But once we cross that line, fear creates a landslide.

Each defective belief produces more defective cells. That makes a lot of sense, doesn't it? You have a day filled with fear—does your body produce healthy cells or does it produce defective cells? You sleep with too many women and feel guilty—good cells or bad cells? After many years of guilt or fear, you've got an abundance of deformed cells. Have you crossed the threshold yet?

What causes a lack of oxygen in the first place? The fear and constrictive beliefs that alienate you from your light body. Perhaps you've got a family member or friend who had testicular cancer. Now you're so afraid of getting it that you mentally and physically tighten and constrict that area of your body to try to keep the cancer out. Or perhaps you are afraid of the sexual energy of your testicles and your second chakra, so you've clamped down on that energy, refusing to allow it to flow. Either way, you're not allowing yourself to breathe into that area, and you're not allowing the energy to flow. Good cells or bad?

Cancer is a deficiency disease: deficiency of energetic balance, deficiency of light, deficiency of oxygen, deficiency of nutrients and elements, and therefore a deficiency of waste elimination at the cellular level. When you are in this type of deficiency mode, what you eat hardly matters, because nothing goes in or out of your cells!

The Doctor vs. the Self

Do you believe in the doctor or in yourself? Which is your strongest reality? If you're not sure, then stick with your doctor. Otherwise, you must trust yourself and teach yourself to know yourself. You are always the best judge of what is going on inside you.

Doctors treat symptoms. You treat the root. You, when you have cultivated sensitivity, will instinctively know where the problem originated. You will see the energetic and emotional imbalance that has created the lack within your physical form. Now would be the perfect time to understand why the energetic and emotional imbalance continues, and correct it.

Disease is created by your restrictive beliefs and chakra blocks, and constructed by your body. This is one way that you learn about your power to create and manifest. After you merge with your fear in the desire to play it through—to see what it looks like as a physical manifestation—your body first creates deficiency in that area of the body, mixes it with toxicity, and then allows the parasites and bacteria to take over. The organ or part of your body that becomes diseased is based on your particular chakra patterns and beliefs. Where do you constrict your energy?

If you are afraid of deep emotion or suppress your joy within your heart chakra, you will manifest heart disease. If you are afraid to speak out or embrace the self-expression of your throat chakra, you will manifest diseases in your throat and thyroid.

Bacteria and parasites are cocreators of disease—your partners. They simply do what you ask and allow them to do. They assist you in creating your reality. They are always present in your system.

If you believe in doctors, then you give them the upper hand. Together, the two of you explore your *disbelief* in the sovereignty of the individual while the doctor hacks out pieces of your physical creation. Any "medicine" can work miracles if you put sufficient belief—which is energy—into it. But the miracle will only be temporary until you are done with "medicine" and see past all beliefs and static systems.

Healing is nothing more than the allowing of a greater flow of energy throughout the body as you remove your blocks and narrow perceptions—the diseases of your mind—and reconnect with your light body. Can you turn off your thoughts and fears just long enough to hear what your body is saying to you? If not, then it may have to scream at you. This is what disease is.

We are afraid of letting go of what we know in order to venture into uncharted territory. But uncharted territory is where we find the answers to the questions to which we don't have answers. If we already had answers to our problems, then they wouldn't be problems, would they?

A problem is an opportunity to let go of the familiar and go forward into uncharted territory, to freefall into freedom. The choice to use these frightening situations as springboards into the Source is what turns them into challenges instead of disasters, or opportunities instead of failures.

The Hawk

The trees along the side of the winding back street near the small wetlands glistened as the late-morning sunlight ignited their spectacular fall colors. My body loves the deep lazy stillness of this time of year. The air is heavier and thicker, and the blue of the sky is deeper and closer. I slowed my car down to take it all in.

While looking intently at the rapture all around me, my eyes registered a swift and deliberate movement ahead. A bird on the side of the road had shifted in one motion from a standstill on the ground to 12 feet up into an almost barren tree. Fortunately, I was quiet enough inside to hear the voice that told me that I needed to pay attention to what had just occurred.

I leaned over my steering wheel in order to peer out the very top of my windshield into the tree as I slowed down even more. There, perched powerfully on a barren branch, was a fully erect hawk with a broad, brown-spotted chest. He was looking directly at me, fully cognizant of what I had just witnessed. It was as if he had planned the whole event, performed it, and then waited to see if I had been aware enough to catch it. My light body told me that this was no ordinary event.

The hawk had not taken off with the usual flapping of wings in order to get off the ground. He had simply shot straight up in one complete motion from the grass to 12 feet up into the tree with no effort whatsoever. In the two seconds that it took for my body to process the sequence fully, I recalled that a black bird-shaped object had hooked itself to the branch up in the tree, and then allowed itself to be pulled directly up into the tree as if yanked by a string. His path was a direct line, not an arc.

9

Tuning the Physical Body

Your body is a spectacular machine, like a fine car. There is no mystery to it once you understand how it works and you become aware of its various moods, needs, and signals. Then it doesn't just suddenly break down and leave you stranded somewhere. Your body is energy and matter—energy in matter. A powerful light body requires a powerful vehicle, and it needs powerful resources to build and maintain it.

Your physical body holds its youthful suppleness and core strength, resisting your attempts to break it down prematurely with bad habits, until you're in your thirties and your youthful energy starts to wane. Then, seemingly quite unexpectedly, it starts to fall apart. Flaccid core muscles, structural misalignment, tingling sensations in your back, pressure in your rectal area, foggy thoughts, or loss of your usual vigor and vitality are the early warning signs that your bad habits are finally taking their toll on what you thought was your immortal body. It is *not* normal to get a cold or flu every year; it is *sub*normal.

It wasn't until I began maintaining my body *by myself* that I realized how important self-power and self-reliance truly are. You are taking charge of your creation and not asking someone else, such as your doctor, to help you put back together what you willfully took apart. It is the acceptance of your responsibility for the totality of your existence. It is the realization that it's all up to you and that your desire to seek help outside yourself is really a shifting of your responsibility to someone else.

When I was a young lad, my body could only heal itself of colds, flus, or other injuries at night. But now it heals itself in the daytime when I'm awake. My healing is now done *consciously* instead of unconsciously. I make it happen.

When you begin hand-preparing all of your own food, you will come to understand how important it is to have food made with your own energetic intention, and not the weak, bored, frustrated, or fearful energy of an underpaid clerk at a restaurant or store. This process is about *degrees* of energy and *shades* of clarity—pennies in the jar.

The crucial factor in the maintenance of the physical form is a relaxed mind. It doesn't matter if you invest every ounce of energy you have in following perfect dietary guidelines, immaculate cleanliness, or meticulous disinfection. If your brain is stressed out, you talk too much, and your chakras are repressed or overused, *nothing* will heal your body. All maladies are the result of a loss of union between your light body and your physical body. Disease within the body is severance from the Source—your own light body.

There are countless ways to tune the physical body. Very few people have been taught anything of real value when it comes to caring for the physical vehicle. You might have to undergo a thorough transformation, not just of your diet, but of your relationship to your light body and your beliefs.

I have included the methods that worked for me. *Yours may be totally different.* Follow your intuition. Even though the physical manifests from the energetic, you may have some physical problems that need direct correction.

For example, some key channels in my liver were plugged and my system was very sluggish. So I flushed the stones out of my liver and my whole body relaxed and started flowing better. The bacterial and parasitic overload was easily reduced at that point.

A condition that's out of control needs to be addressed

from the inside and the outside simultaneously. Topical treatment only does not eliminate the underlying root.

While it is important to focus and clean the body properly, be vigilant about not getting caught up in the fear associated with any method. The important thing is to allow the knowledge to assist you in making conscious choices about your body, not fear-based reactions.

Know that fear can actually be *more* toxic than any chemical or junk food. Fear binds the negative or deleterious aspects of *anything* to your body. Otherwise, toxins would simply pass right through your system. Fear unbalances your poles and makes nasty things stick to you. Remember that fear is a binding force; it is your own creative energy being used to create negative situations for you to learn and grow from.

Your physical body can become worn out, however, if imbalances or negativity constantly surround you and you cannot sustain your vigilance. Then your body wears out prematurely and falters, and toxins bind to your cells.

Monatomic elements are drained from your system when fear and stress set in. Then your physical body becomes more disconnected from your light body. More disconnection equals more decay. And more decay equals less consciousness and less awareness.

The Dual Nature of Your Organs

Digestion, assimilation, elimination, and cleansing are the lower functions of your organs. Their higher function is the sensing of subtle energies flowing from other people, animals, and the Earth. This information is relayed to your chakras and your brain. Cleaning out and sensitizing your body and organs greatly enhances their higher functions.

My perineum and anus detect your receptivity to physical existence and tell me whether or not you are fully grounded in your body. My genitals tell me what you use your sexual energy for. My kidneys detect the fear in your kidneys. My liver detects the anger and frustration in your liver. My heart feels your joy or fear of joy. My lungs sense your grief, my throat your fear of expression or overindulgence, my third eye your refusal to hear your light body, and my activated brain sees the strength of your connection to the Source.

Cleaning the Inside of the Body

A kidney cleanse helps to get out the stones or crystals, and ensures that your body is capable of easily eliminating any toxins that are released as you go through other processes. Use herbs to kill an overabundance of parasites. Liver cleanses remove gallstones. Gallstones only get backed up into the gall-bladder *after* your liver is already full of them. An electronic, frequency generating Zapper will help to kill off bacteria and parasites. The information for these protocols can be found in *The Cure for All Diseases,* by Hulda Clark.

Kill This, Kill That

The usual tendency is to focus on being antibacterial instead of pro-immune and pro good bacteria. Focus less on the antidisease angle and more on the life-giving joy of living and working in conjunction with the microscopic life forms that can assist you in building a strong body and mind. In this situation, everybody wins. Then your body will be completely capable of taking care of any invaders or imbalances.

Killing off bad bacteria and fungus seems like a good idea, but remember that your body has its own wisdom. If you have an overgrowth of bacteria, fungus, or yeast, such as *Candida,* then your body has entered into a symbiotic relationship with this microorganism because it provides something that your body needs but is not getting in a low-oxygen and low-circulation area. So the microorganism is allowed to proliferate.

Find out *why* your body required this symbiotic relationship in the first place. Prematurely eradicating the yeast, for one, may actually be more harmful to your health than if you allow it to exist while you find out why your body has entered into this relationship. Build up your immune system in the mean time.

If you need or crave something that is "bad" for you, such as sugar, you can't take it away without replacing the thing or emotion that your body needs. Your body has wisdom, even if it seems misguided. It looks around at what you have, or at what you *allow* yourself to have, and then figures out how it can get what it needs to survive.

If you deny your system its natural exhilaration and joy by stifling the spontaneity of your light body, then you will crave sugar or chocolate to bring an artificial "pleasure" to your system—a pleasure that has consequences. Caffeine becomes necessary when an exhausted system needs to be pushed to do a job that it despises. You crave starches when parasites have the upper hand.

Sofa King Clean

Note: Please refer to Resources and Suggested Reading for companies assisting with the products mentioned here.

Our environment is a toxic mess. Trying to escape the slow and insipid toxification from the chemicals in home building products, foam furniture, carpets, water, and crop spraying is practically impossible. Everywhere you turn someone is gassing you with some crap. It's truly amazing that our bodies hold up as well as they do amidst all of this. It's really a testament to their potential if they are treated well. Think of all the miracles waiting to happen if we'd only optimize our bodies instead of permitting them to get dumped on.

Your body cannot detoxify itself if you keep cramming more toxins into it. It is probably already overloaded. Things such as bleach, detergents, soaps, household chemicals, foam bedding and furniture, non-organic clothing (especially underwear and socks), toilet paper, nose tissues, and other paper products whitened with chlorine and contaminated with dioxins (the major cause of hemorrhoids and toxic shock syndrome), hair gels, rubbing alcohol, toothpaste, deodorant, tap and bottled water, metal utensils and cookware, colognes, shaving creams, antacids, hairdryers, fluorescent lights, computers, and microwaves are all toxic to your system. Try a good ionic hair dryer, Ott-Lite full spectrum light bulbs, and organic, unbleached (or hydrogen peroxide bleached) body products and clothes. Bottled water almost always has some kind of mold growing in it, or is contaminated by chlorine leaching from the plastic bottle. Look into a good water filter instead.

I started eating organic, biodynamic, and non–genetically modified foods to get away from neurotoxins and pesticides. Our society is practically blind to the reality of where its food comes from and how it is processed. I could write a book on why I did these things, but you can read one of the many out there and find out for yourself. Toxins have an adverse or dulling effect on the sensitivity and receptivity of the entire physical organism.

And what's the deal with soap? In the Bible, God tells the Israelites that if they accidentally crap on themselves or on their friends they should bathe in water and run around until nightfall screaming "Unclean!" If the Israelites survived on plain old water, then why do we suddenly need soap?

Regular soap doesn't even kill bacteria. It only loosens the protective oils on the skin that might harbor bacteria so that they can be rinsed off. Antibacterial soap kills germs, but antibacterial soap contains toxins that have to be sent to your liver to be broken down and removed from your already overtaxed system.

It turns out that water and air used to contain higher concentrations of ozone and hydrogen peroxide, and were very powerful purifiers and rejuvenators—the best. Both ozone and diluted food-grade hydrogen peroxide are natural oxidizers and will kill off the parasites and bacteria that can only survive in low-oxygen environments. Diluted food-grade hydrogen peroxide also eats up dead organic material (like dead skin), thereby cleansing the body, but does not harm healthy cells unless you spill it undiluted on your skin or in your eyes. I've also found it to be helpful with weird moles, cysts, bumps, rashes, fungus, blackheads, and dark hair.

If you drink ozonated water, or *one drop* of food-grade hydrogen peroxide in a cup of water, it will help to oxygenate your system, and then come out of your pores and kill off whatever crud is growing on your skin, or in your armpits or crotch. Molecularly restructured water assists in permeating cell walls and flushing them out. You may experience side effects as the oxygen, diluted peroxide, and water clean out your cells.

Don't ever be in a rush to detoxify your system. It is a slow, deliberate, and often uncomfortable process. It can cause nervousness, agitation, all kinds of foul body odors, and headaches, plus it makes you want to come out of your body. But these things are signals that the process is working. If you are unsure of the process or are uncomfortable, seek guidance. Always trust that inner voice.

A good weekly, or monthly, soaking in diluted food-grade hydrogen peroxide will cleanse the skin—your largest organ—and keep you smelling fresh and feeling smooth all over. Diluted food-grade hydrogen peroxide works wonders for bleaching laundry without harming you or the environment.

Diet

I loathe vegetables. Many times I crammed the varieties of "good" vegetables down my throat, only to wind up ten pounds lighter and ravenously hungry with flaming stains on my shorts. Then I'd get various rashes on my hands and feet. My body just could not utilize or assimilate raw vegetables. For my body, they are an imperfect food source.

I tried every way of cooking them, even smothering them with gallons of cheese. But it was all to no avail. The only vegetables I liked were carrots and peas. The only food I craved was steak with a side order of meat and a beef-shake. Finally, a genius turned me on to raw milk. From there I found raw cheese, raw cultured kefir, fil mjölk (a culture from Sweden), yogurt, sprouted grains, nuts, seeds, lacto-fermented flours and grains, and, finally, fermented vegetables.

Maybe you've heard that lame derisive line: "Humans are

the only mammals that keep drinking milk after they're weaned"? Well, it's a bunch of crap. Our ancestors in practically all cultures made use of milk throughout their entire lives, whether from cows, sheep, yaks, mares, or camels. They made curds, whey, beers, fermented vegetables and fruits, yogurt, kefir, and cheese. They used the animals' stomachs or intestines for storing and culturing. And those barbarians were some hefty hombres.

You may say, "But, dude, what about all that dairy? Doesn't it clog you up and give you the squirts?" No. That's just it. Back when I was eating cooked or pasteurized dairy, I did have problems. Back when I was just throwing beans in a pot for an hour, or making bread from yeast, I did have problems.

But once I got cleaned up and then started in with the raw milk, butter, cream, cheese, and cultured vegetables, everything clicked. By using raw whey to ferment grains and legumes, I could even eat beans without blowing the door off the house—not even a whimper or a gurgle! I started making bread without yeast. And the best part is that once I found the raw and fermented foods, my body finally said, "This is what we've been craving all these years." Wow.

Fermentation breaks down the inassimilable components, unlocks hidden energetic properties, and perfects the food. Our ancestors shredded up fresh cabbage, threw in some salt, stomped on it, put it in crocks, and let it ferment. Then they put it in cold storage to let it "ripen" or cure. They fermented many types of vegetables and fruits, meats, condiments, and dairy. Fermented food is high in *Lactobacillus* and live enzymes crucial to a healthy gut and superior digestion. Fermentation also produces hydrogen peroxide.

Our modern pasteurized versions of these ancient foods are *dead*. Other modern varieties of these foods made with vinegar are also *dead*. There are no live enzymes to help with digestion. This means that your body has to expend its own enzymes, thereby weakening it and eventually leading to problems with digestion and putrefaction.

I eat organic red meat when my body gets too lean and craves fat, or when it gets really cold outside. Sometimes I ferment the meat without cooking it. Otherwise, I eat organic chicken that's been cooked in a slow cooker for about nine hours to help extract more nutrients. I add lots of molecularly restructured water, use dark meat cuts with the bones and skin included, and have the butcher cut the bones in half. This makes for a really dense and rich broth. Boneless, skinless cuts with no cartilage are deficient in vital nutrients.

Fats and oils are crucial to your body's health, whether from meat, dairy, nuts, or seeds. Each body has different requirements, so find what works well for you. Remember that foods are color-coded for your convenience. Try to eat some of each, and flow with the changes that each season brings.

I also keep my food pretty bland, and I've come to enjoy the natural flavors of the foods themselves, with the occasional addition of Celtic Sea Salt. Now, even the smallest amounts of chocolate or caffeine can keep me up all night. Moderate portions of easily digestible foods increase the time and strength available to your body for other things, like being conscious throughout your sleep.

Your body has to like and agree with your dietary changes. Otherwise it will just get stressed out, and then you will be cranky and have dragon breath. If your body doesn't like certain changes, then you may have parasites or some other deficiency. If your body is getting what it needs—and it's not the voice of the parasites speaking—then you will know it and you will feel very solid and content.

You need a balance of energies. So eat meat with some fermented vegetables and raw milk, if it suits you. Then you get a balance of living vibrations coupled with the animal spirit energy. Try a little aloe juice before meals to help heal your digestive system and colon. Or eat lightly steamed vegetables with raw organic butter if that's what your body craves.

All fear-based diets damage the body, regardless of how organic, vegan, or properly prepared they are. Food is important, but your beliefs are more important. Fear is more toxic than pesticides. Your primary food is light and breath, flowing without obstruction.

Be wary of pills of any kind, regardless of their purity. Digestion begins in the mouth. If you want your body to absorb nutrients, then those nutrients have to mingle with saliva. Pills bypass saliva and get mostly pissed out, or they accumulate in your kidneys and form crystals. Or they may go into your stomach and create some kind of gas or bloating because they haven't mingled with saliva. If you're determined to take pills, then chew them first. If you drink a wheatgrass shot or take a spoonful of cod liver oil, leave it in your mouth until your saliva turns it to water, then swallow it.

Pain

Sometimes when there is pain in the body, it is a sign that something is being worked on, or that something is finally releasing. We have a tendency to immediately think that something is broken or defective, and proceed to anesthetize, immobilize, or cut out the problem instead of being patient and allowing the body to work its wisdom and cleanse itself. Fear only inhibits the process. Look for the emotional and energetic contributions, not just the physical.

Fitness

If your muscles are tight, it may not mean that they need stretching. It may mean that other muscles need strengthening so that they can take some of the load off the tight muscles. Then the tight muscles can relax. Classical Pilates worked wonders for my body, strengthening muscles I never knew I had, and opening up deep channels. Deep Yin Yoga is also a good choice.

Get outside often and move around, play, or exercise. Otherwise, with all this inner focus, you'll go absolutely bonkers.

Consuming Consciousness

Monatomic elements have existence in both the physical and energetic worlds, simultaneously. So do regular food and water. Therefore the energy coming from your beliefs, attitudes, and fears *directly* affects the quality of your food and water. If your physical body is filled with light, it needs less physical food because it is being fed from your Source.

Consciousness *is* food. Every life form consumes a lower form of consciousness to survive. Bugs eat plants. Cows eat bugs and grass. We eat cows. Other energies consume our fear and emotional spikes. We are part of the chain of consciousness. The Source feeds off of all of us.

The Earth is our source of physical life, our partner in this part of the journey. As physical beings, we are required to take life from the Earth if we desire to continue our physical existence. Life feeds on life. Whether it is from plants or animals—or even if it is just water or air—we take life from the Earth to continue our own. This is part of the physical dance. We consume energy to beget energy. We assimilate awareness to enhance our own awareness.

The thing to remember is to tread lightly and not be greedy or careless with this life. Always give thanks to the forms of life that give of themselves so that you may continue. Give back by evolving yourself. Then you will be capable of caring for the Earth and all of its many forms of life with respect.

The House

"Here I am at this creepy old house again," I think to myself, as I am drawn up the stairs from the large grassy area to the porch. It is pitch-black, except for some kind of chilling gray glow around each window and door. This entity is two stories tall and made of heavy, dark lumber planks. It has a Gothic or Victorian flair to it, and the night hangs close around each of the dim yellow bulbs that sporadically illuminate the porch circling it. I have been here many times before.

But something is more potent this time. I move into the narrow and strangely suffocating hallway. The ceiling is 12 feet high, with lots of nooks filled with old books, or high-up cupboard doors that bow out under the bulk of the spirits lurking within.

"This house is alive," I hiss deep inside, afraid that it might know that I know.

The walls pulse and heave with breath, following my own and amplifying it within and without. Everything is extremely vivid and corporeal, warm and sensual.

I make my way heavily down the hallway, passing a large wood-framed window on my right. Inside is what looks like a large dining hall with an enormous but barren solid wood table. The eerie gray glow surrounds the window, and its unnerving cavernous current almost draws me in.

But something is pulling me on, again with the suffocation, and now the heat becomes thick like water. The walls are draped in heavy linens, with embroidered scallops hanging from the high-up ceiling. These linens conceal haunting memories of lives from long ago and worlds that have no relevance here, just as this house has no business being here.

Powers from other worlds and past lives lick at my elbows and knees, and my bowels churn with fear and excitation. The motion slows, and I am turned all the way around until I am almost facing forward again, except that I am facing the left wall. I am off the ground, levitating, pulsing with power, completely enthralled by the breath coming from behind a veil near the ceiling. Something is shaped like an enormous grandfather clock that reaches all the way to the floor—heavy, wide, eerie, enveloping, and too present. I am terrified to my bones, but thrilled to death to be finally close to it. I feel myself waking up in the dream.

I reach out and grab the paper veil covering the face. My hand tingles with electricity. I yank the paper off and the eyes sizzle and sputter as they blaze out and drill into my frozen, hovering form. The hair stands up all over my head, and my testicles pull up tight against my groin. My sphincter dilates and discharges energy as the current bursts down into my legs, lighting up the bottoms of my feet as they dangle in midair, wave after wave of chills sweeping up and down my spine.

10

Power

*Meditation is not something you practice
—it is a way of life.*

Meditation

Watching the last of the yellowed leaves being blown from the sleeping birch tree, I wondered how anyone could ever deny himself the peace and silence of a morning such as this by rushing around being busy while the Earth is sleeping. I wanted nothing more than to curl up in a warm chair with my hot food and stare—stare without a single thought in my head. In the distance, the fiery maples teased the evergreen pines with their rapture. "I love you" is the only thing that came to my mind.

Real meditation is not a system or something foreign to the rest of your life. It is a natural trance state, an elixir. A mind filled with its unresolved past or bulging with unconfronted fear cannot be forced to be silent without some kind of backlash or repercussion.

It's not as if one day you suddenly have no more chatter in your head. It's just that the chatter moves further and further away, and no longer consumes you. Be always vigilant so as not to engage or nurture any thought.

For your light body to merge fully with your physical

body, you must first empty your physical body and mind of blocks, fears, and the past. Your mind becomes still because your life becomes simple and you focus on the Source. If you are busy all of the time, your mind will reflect that, and trying to quiet it is a sheer waste of time.

How can you ever find silence if you talk ceaselessly to others or to yourself? Allow your thoughts to come and go, and don't feed them with made-up conversations or "what-if" scenarios. *Listen* instead to the voice of your light body. When you listen, you are feeling the universe, and you will suddenly find yourself understanding and communicating with everything and everyone.

If I am not still and restful on the days when I need absolute quiet—on highly meditative days—I get extremely irritated and agitated. My body wants to be quiet, to remain in its extra-low-frequency state. It is refueling itself, reconnecting to its Source. My brain is expanding, becoming filled with Light.

Slow down and simplify, and you will be able to give the utmost attention to the smallest detail. This is how you wake up in your dreams, how you meditate throughout your day, how your mind becomes quick and sensitive enough to hear your light body. Here's where your two worlds meet. Meditation is a place.

Recapitulation

The Pythagoreans practiced recapitulation twice per day, in the morning and at night, to clear the mind and still the sleep. They simply sat quietly and reviewed the events of that day or night. Pythagoras was trained in the Egyptian mystery schools.

Recapitulation is about shifting dimensions and playing with time. You learn to re-access your past in a real way. The act of recollecting your past seems on the outside to be an exercise in memory recall. But it is so much more than that. You are learning to recall *all* of the frequencies that made up the event, not just the visual. By allowing your body to recall smells, sounds, tastes, images, impressions, and the emotions associated with past events, what you are actually doing is training your organs and chakras to perform memory recall just as you've trained your brain.

In the daily world, your eyes, ears, nose, body, brain, chakras, and organs focus on the energy that flows through them in a very intense and unwavering manner. Your physical reality is created by your decision to hold or *stabilize* certain energetic currents from among the many that flow around and through you. Physical reality is a *consensus dream*. That's why it is so engaging; there are so many people doing it at the same time and in the same way. Once you store sufficient energy, however, you can choose to focus on one of the more subtle, or less intense, realities; you establish your own consensus reality. You are learning to *create* the reality of your choice, instead of being told which reality to create.

Multiconscious states are glimpsed when you eradicate preconceived ideas about energy and learn not to prejudge what your organs and chakras perceive. But these multiconscious states can only be solidified if you have trained your entire being to hold those subtle and elusive energies in the same way that you have learned to hold them in your daily life. *Hold* the image. *Hold* the smell. *Hold* the feeling.

Recapitulation is the deliberate act of accessing previously played out energetic currents by directing your focus toward these more subtle currents. The past—your past—consists of subtle currents that you have already played once before. But perhaps you didn't play those currents to the best of your ability, or according to your highest desire. And so those currents linger, still attached to your very being.

Your past is one such subtle current. So is your future. And so are the other realities going on around you all of the time. The ability to focus your entire being on these more subtle currents is what *creates* and *solidifies* other realities—the world of ghosts, for example.

There is no procedure to recapitulation other than sitting quietly, allowing a memory to surface, and then directing your focus at it until it solidifies. Practice is your greatest asset.

This is how you will realize that your past can be altered. By changing your energetic *relationship* to your past, you modify the energetic outcome and change your present. Awareness is eternal, a layer *over* time, not within time. Your awareness affects the world.

Recapitulation is also about the assimilation and processing of the energy that you ignored or repressed at the time of the event. Your fear squashed the deep emotion, and now it's locked down inside you. Learn to pay attention to the feelings and energy directed at you *in the moment* so that there is no residue left over to affect your mind and body in your present or as you sleep.

If your brain does not let go of past memories, it will eventually become too full to listen to your light body and to the energetic or "psychic" information coming from the worlds around you. The same is true of your internal organs. Your internal organs retain the feelings associated with past events. Part of recapitulation involves the release of the repressed emotion associated with the memory. Then you learn to recognize the fear and its trigger.

You must only be a witness to your recapitulation—a passive, nonjudgmental, nonpartisan witness. *Observe* the process, the memories arising from deep within your bones and organs. Merge with, assimilate, and then release the past. This will set you, and those you have interacted with, free.

Recapitulation heightens inner focus and control. It's an exercise in learning how to refine the subtle clasping of energetic currents. This holding is what allows consciousness to flow back and forth from sleeping to waking, or from your subconscious to your consciousness. It's an exercise in frequency matching. When you return your body and mind to the exact frequency of the original event, you suddenly "remember" the emotions, smells, tastes, sounds, and sights of that event.

Recapitulation helps develop the front part of the brain, and enhances the connection between the center of the brain, the chakras, emotions, and the third eye. It is this network that is primarily used in maintaining consciousness in sleep.

Power

Passivity only works in a vacuum, or where forces have no volition or harmful intention. But in the real world, you need power to stand up to power—you need power to consume the darkness. Be cocky while everyone waits desperately for you to blow it big time. Be confident in the face of everyone else's disbelief in the power of originality, and pull it off anyway—with gusto. Convert the disbelievers into fans.

This type of confidence has been lost in our shoddy little world. People want to believe that it's always up to some force outside their control. It's a nice excuse for those who continually fail. Fear is their god. We could use a few people who are just sick and tired of the same old dipshit stuff. Somebody needs to pull it off in front of everybody else.

Those afraid of affection and vulnerability commune with powers of a lesser nature. They attempt to buttress themselves with animal spirits, ghosts, angry foreign energies, or reptiles. Energy matches your intention; it is impersonal. It will reinforce whatever you believe and dedicate yourself to, whether it's creative or destructive.

People too chickenshit to stick their necks out and pursue their own dreams in front of everybody else are the first cowards to criticize those who muster enough courage to take a chance. These backstabbers turn their own fear of making mistakes and failing outward onto others, attempting to bring them down. The presence of success would only make everyone more aware of how spineless these pathetic cowards truly are.

Darkness and destruction are born of fear, and fear is resistance to life. Therefore, one who is *not* resistant to life and who harbors no fear has the *potential* to wield more power. Creative aggression has infinite potential.

From Little to Big

When you detach yourself sufficiently from your senses and restrictive beliefs, finding your magnificence becomes more important than immediate gratification. This is the only way for you to be able to see beyond your little world and into a bigger picture. Here is where you recognize the significance of your investment in power over time—years, not days or minutes.

The motivation for immediate gratification of the senses is driven by a fear of loss, a fear of being denied or of never having the object that brings you pleasure. If food was used to coerce you into behaving as a child, then that fear of never having enough food or enough of its pleasures is what motivates your desire for immediate gratification now. Hence the attachment to food.

If you were denied pleasure as a youth, or if you denied yourself pleasure for a religion or some belief, then this leads to a reaction now. You are afraid of being denied again, so you hoard your pleasures. So don't deny yourself anything—get it out of your system without harming yourself or others—but be very awake as you walk through the release of your fear of being denied.

Retaining Power

When you experience power and you are weak, your tendency will be to give your power up. When you see a powerful woman, you say she's hot and you want her. But ultimately what you want is to dribble your own power out inside of her. Then she becomes more powerful than you.

If this weren't true, then you would ravish her and retain your seed for yourself. Then you would get to see her lust for power, or its opposite, firsthand. She would desire you again and again until, in your exhaustion, you gave it up. Or she might dump you because you were not "there for her." Or she might just submit to you in order to be led by the hand through life.

You are so turned on by power that it excites your energy and makes your energy want to run out in response to that power. You need self-control or, even better, a desire not to be ruled by others or their power. You need a desire to be master of your own destiny. Desire not to be a slave to anyone else's power. Set your own course. Or at least be an equal, and enjoy the give and take of a partnership.

Stop giving away your power to others because you are afraid to create or live your own reality. Look at the masses that want someone to tell them what to do. They hang onto the feet of the priest, the politician, the doctor, the author, the recording artist, or the movie star, begging them to tell them what to do or show them how to live. Everyone knows what it feels like to follow the leader, but how many know what it feels like to be in front?

You are free to be totally mysterious and unpredictable, the man behind the scenes. Don't be afraid to stand up in front of everyone and bare your ass. You will feel very alone, vulnerable, and naked. You have taken a stand and no one is supporting you—*not yet.* But while you're standing there butt-naked in front of the world, have the courage to bend over and grab the Source by the ankles and pull it up into yourself while everyone is watching!

Loneliness is not a lack of companionship. It is, rather, your unwillingness to allow your own energy to *fill up the space surrounding you.* You have inhibited your self-expression, self-development, and self-actualization. Once you allow yourself to unlock your energy, it will blossom before your very eyes, and people will seek your company before you seek theirs.

When your chakras attain a state of harmony, there is uninhibited flow. Uninhibited flow is boundless energy, and boundless energy is power. So harmony is actually the harnessing of power. Self-love is the realization of power.

Self-Esteem and Ignorance

If you see someone do something that is repugnant to you,

say something. You don't need to yell or scream or get violent. Just approach that person and tell them matter-of-factly that the way they are acting or treating another is disrespectful and ignorant. If you don't do or say something, then you have allowed ignorance to continue in the world.

Potential

Stagnant energy is poverty.

You fight to be free. You get angry and rise up, but become suddenly afraid of your own strength. You distract yourself with drama or sedate the whole mess with drugs. Power is screaming at you, telling you that you *are* the light, not just a vehicle for light. You have to listen, but you are caught up in the little "you." And so that energy turns sour, becoming depression, rage, violence, disease, and then death without fulfillment.

What is your future? It is everything you don't perfect today, every fear you don't face, every situation you run from, and every love you don't pursue. The future is only as predictable as you are. Are you thoroughly predictable? Cultivate your renegade spirit.

Show your intention with *action* and the Source will match your commitment. Taking a stand is manifesting energetic Truth in the physical world. Taking a stand sends shock waves throughout the physical dream and wakes people up.

Taking a stand *necessarily* polarizes the energies around you. Don't be tossed to and fro by those currents. Decide who you are and divide the current in two. Hold nothing back. Make fearless love to fearful people. If you hold back in fear of the negative or harmful intentions of others, you are stating that they are more powerful than you, that their negativity can override your positivity.

Wielding Power

The ones who accuse others of being power mongers are the ones who are so afraid of their own power or inability to wield it that they'd rather bring others down to their own half-assed level. This is not about having power for the sake of lording it over others; it's about the development of your third chakra and then balancing that power with the energy of the other chakras in order to be a complete human being at the height of your form. Don't be half-assed about it—use your whole ass. Act as if you believe it until you actually do.

Energy goes forth from your eyes toward an object or person. When that energy reaches the "polite" safety limit that has been arbitrarily set, you reel it back in. But the energy of your eyes and chakras can do so much more. When your energy is bold and strong, it can go deep inside another person, graciously penetrating their resistance to joy. Fear and the culture of respectability are what stop your energy from flowing into and through all people and things.

Don't avoid things out of fear. Instead, make choices based on your deepest feelings. Use your desire to create the greatest power. Bring through your essence and unleash your potential for others to see. Believe in yourself enough to let the necessary amount of energy loose to create phenomenal results.

There was a time when I was afraid to make the first move in case nobody else liked it or wanted to come along. I was afraid of letting others know my plans ahead of time, afraid to commit, afraid of my purpose, and afraid of being thought less of if I pushed for what I wanted. I was afraid to stand up for what I felt in case I was ridiculed. I was afraid to trust that I would be taken care of, for fear that I might be disappointed and lose faith in myself and the Source. It was safer to be a fence-sitter.

Now I want it all, the best of everything. Creative aggression is the only way to make things happen. Passivity is for the dogs. Pursue what you want and this will put the energy out there. *Listen* to your light body, then *act*. Physical existence is aggression. The act of acquiring energy is aggressive. Taking any kind of life—plant or animal—to enhance your own is aggressive.

You can change *any* situation at *any* time if you don't flinch. The strength of your conviction is what determines your effectiveness. When you are filled from the Source, then power and affection flow outward and lift others. When you are empty inside, you become a human vacuum, sucking the energy out of everyone you come into contact with.

Anyone or anything can rob you of power if you allow it to, but not otherwise. Even in a battle, there is always a point where one opponent energetically releases, allowing the other to rise up. Your self-induced conscious or unconscious weakness coupled with your fearful projection will create whatever thought you hold in your mind at that moment. It's always up to you. Physical strength *seems* to be a factor and can be intimidating. But awareness and the strength of your connection to your light body are the ultimate.

Use the world to gauge if your perceptions of energy are accurate or skewed. Put yourself out there, mouth off a little bit, and see what comes back to you. It will be a gift of enhanced self-knowing.

And don't shy away from people who are more aggressive than you are. Embrace them, and quickly shatter your fear. Aggressive people make you uncomfortable, push your buttons, and quickly reveal the things you are trying to hide or protect. They put you on a stand and look up your shorts, revealing all of your nasty little secrets. Be fearless and lovingly ruthless with yourself. Then you will always see clearly.

You as the Creator

We need to be aware of our thoughts. Where did they come from? Why are they here? Are they my own? Become aware of how you respond to them, interact with them, feed them. Choose not to. Choose silence. Choose space. The Source rides in the space between your thoughts.

Other energies cannot work with us until we become aware of their presence. Otherwise they are just some random nebulous feeling or "wind." But perhaps one day, your mind is exceptionally quiet and your usual belief systems are in the bathroom taking a dump, and suddenly a wind blows by you and you register that it has a unique identity, a persona. Then later, it leaves the impression of a name inside you. And you then tell someone that name and describe the feeling. Now that other person is aware of it, too. The persona is fed by your combined focus, and it *becomes more solid, more tangible.*

We are trying to create God in the flesh. Your light body desires to manifest a miracle of awareness out of physical matter. Your physical body is your beliefs given life; it is your creation on display, the result of your power. This *is* Genesis—this *is* creation. We are the miracle.

The Source has given us the power to create as we see fit. We have been given the ability to seed the Earth. How far does this go? Do you realize that your thoughts seed the Earth, too? Are you aware that every word from your mouth kindles energetic forces that compose and relay information and feelings throughout all energetic worlds? Someday you will seed your own universe. But, for now, you already have one.

The Van

One winter afternoon, my girlfriend Susan and I were in southern California driving north on the 405 freeway just before where 101 splits off. It was a fairly warm and lazy day, and I was in somewhat of a trance coming down the grade. Things were starting to pile up as they always do at this junction, with people trying to sneak in at the last minute and others swerving out of the congested lanes to try to cram themselves back in again farther ahead. I had slowed down quite a bit, leaving plenty of room for those behaving badly to do what they had to do, when I noticed something threatening occurring in the lane immediately to my left.

The people were all following too closely when a few

more cars jammed themselves back in. A guy in a vintage convertible Corvette immediately slowed down for them, but the man behind him in the beat-up white van didn't register it until too late. I saw him stand up and stomp on the brake.

His wheels immediately locked up, and his rear tires laid down a thick black layer of smoking rubber. He cranked the wheel, the back end of his van swerving dangerously out of the lane, and then he jerked the wheel back the other way. The van rocked up onto two wheels. My stomach immediately sank, my senses telling me that this van was falling over onto the side of my car.

My lower abdomen grew extremely hot. The rest of my body went suddenly numb and into autopilot, and everything went into slow motion. A thick blackness surrounded my head as if I was going to pass out. The blackness was shaped like a cloud, and even though it felt like it had come from behind my skull and enveloped my entire head, I could still see just fine; it was superimposed over my vision of the teetering van.

Then this black cloud flew toward the van and merged with another black cloud that raced toward the van at the same time. They surrounded the van like they were some kind of vacuum cushion. The van stalled as the cloud absorbed all of its energy of motion and gravity. The van righted itself and stopped, barely out of its lane about a foot behind the Corvette. None of the jaded Los Angeles drivers were at all fazed, except for the van driver who would've looked like he had just soiled himself had he not been so stoned already. The Corvette driver just barely glanced in his mirror.

After the van stopped, I noticed I was in a deep daze, a timeless state where things seemingly overlapped. In that timelessness, the preceding events were not separate; they had all existed at the same moment. It felt as though time had simply been the instrument used to decide which events went in which order, and somehow time pasted them together with a little fudging in the middle.

11

The Light Body

The Source sought to know itself, and this created a schism; the Source was split in two. The Source became the dreamer and we became its dream, its dream in time. We have done the same thing. Our light bodies—the Source—seek to know themselves, and so create the physical body, our reflection. We are our own dream. The way back is to reunify, to remove the schism, the division between what is conscious and what is unconscious.

Consciousness is the expression in time of your light body. Conscious dreaming signals the merging of your consciousness with the unconscious aspects of your light body. Pursue the world of the light body, and discover the real world of power.

Everything is energy. Thus the Source becomes aware of itself in all its perfection *and* all its distortion. A perfect accountant is one aspect of the Source, as is a perfect asshole or a perfected Being. Spirit is more real than matter, and not the other way around. Your light body is a force. It has volition.

When you *are* your light body, you do not think about yourself or about anything else—you just *are*. By allowing your light body to lead your consciousness, when your consciousness stops trying to figure everything out, you become whole again. Embrace your physicality and merge with your light body. Then you are conscious of both worlds and can play in either. Incorporate the abilities of your light body into your physical experience.

You are immortal. But if you become mortal by identifying only with the physical, then your immortality is lost.

As children, we all had lucid dreams and out-of-body experiences—flying dreams and dreams with other energies. It felt fantastic. As adults, it's only natural that some part of ourselves unconsciously seeks to return to that feeling. But where has that feeling gone?

It is buried in your lost emotions, hidden in your constricted chakras, and lying dormant in your south pole. It is strangled by fear, limited by your beliefs, and just outside the grasp of your frazzled and stressed-out brain. Your physical body and light body are unable to bridge the gap between energy and matter due to a deficiency of monatomic elements.

As a child, you experienced many events related to the world of the light body, but they were energetic events without physical counterparts; they had no existence and no apparent relevance in the world of society and adults. So you learned to separate the two, and consider one real and one not real. So these events remained sub-real, or just beneath your reality. Once you discovered the words with which to describe those sub-real events, however, they were suddenly given substance in the physical world.

Once you are aligned with your light body, its direct input becomes your direct output. There is no processing and no censoring. There is no interpretation or coloration; there is no thought. There is only spontaneous action.

Activating Your Light Body

What makes a moment lush, full, and very real? The moment when your light body is immersed in your physical body. This is called "being in the moment." You had a lot of these moments as a child. Now you have very few. Sex is one of the few moments that this still occurs, but it is fleeting and you wind up draining yourself even more in the process.

If you identify primarily with your physical body, then your light body seems to be a foreign force or something outside yourself. But your light body is your true self—your knowledge and your authority. The ultimate challenge of your light body is to find out how much of itself can be manifested in the physical world. It would resemble an explosion, where the energy of the Source is suddenly freed into the physical world. But because this is a dream in time, it trickles in at a rate determined by your limitations.

I used to get really wound up anticipating the archaeological discoveries of ancient secrets that would reveal the hidden mysteries, once and for all. And then I discovered that I was wasting my time waiting! The hidden Truth *is* your light body and its abilities. The greatest secret is total consciousness—asleep or awake—on all levels and in all worlds. This is freedom and power, joy and the absolute adventure.

But your light body needs to be fed. Feed it with your focus, your love, your sexual energy, your emotions, your order, and your perfected physical body and still mind. Strengthen the connection between your physical body and your light body with monatomic elements. Your light body is your ticket to *all* mysteries—it *is* the ancient buried mystery.

Your light body lives in the present eternal moment. Your mind and your thoughts live everywhere else. Your light body is what influences the energy of matter. Conscious dreaming and out-of-body experiences are only the beginning. You get there by going inside and allowing it to surface.

When your light body is close to your physical body and you focus your attention on something, your light body goes to that something and touches it for you, bringing back a connection and a feeling of knowing.

As you consciously remove the impediments to your journey of awareness, you "recognize" people you have never met, as if you had known them all along. The barriers of individuality and separation start to break down as you see the Source—yourself—in everyone else.

Now all people become something more to you as you begin to see them as receptacles of the Source. Together in this realization, you and they agree to unite as larger, more aware energetic units. This is utopia.

Disengage from your logical mind as much as possible. Thought is nothing more than the rearranging of words, the known. Thought is pabulum for your restless energy. Revelations come when thought is silent and your light body speaks.

Just let yourself be free—free to wander at will, to try or not try things as you feel them out. Eliminate excess and stray ends. Rest, find calm and peace in your chosen living environment, and don't be in a hurry.

Practice following your guts daily. Disconnect from imposed loyalties and attachments, and fear-based beliefs or habits. Be conscious at every moment. Watch your body language, facial expressions, hand gestures, the angle of your stance, the tone and inflection in your voice, and the speed of your delivery. Notice how much more people respect and listen to you if you do not feel harried or frantic. Stay in your body and stay grounded. Feel your feet and wiggle your toes to make sure you're connected to the Earth at all times, especially in public.

Real knowledge comes from the light body and moves into the physical body. Reading can be a great way to trigger hidden knowledge, but so can silence and listening. There is nothing in any book that you don't know already. There is vastly more knowledge and wisdom in your light body than in all the ancient texts in the world.

Meditation is the *act* of listening to your light body. It is not something you do to shut out the world, or to escape from your crappy little existence. The art of listening to your light body is the art of learning to shut the hell up and absorb everything around you. It is the art of hearing the birds, smelling the dew as it basks in the morning sun, feeling the caress of the fresh and light breeze, drinking in the mellow affection of the sun, and noticing the joy in your being because you are alive and at peace.

When you *listen* you are *feeling* the universe. Suddenly, you find yourself understanding and communicating with everything and everyone. This is self-awareness.

We've broken everything into pieces and disconnected ourselves in our fragmentation. Lucid dreaming, out-of-body experiences, remote viewing, dissociation, astral projection, the appearances of angels, intuition, psychic abilities, and multidimensionality all involve the light body. The only difference between them is in the type of action performed by the light body. Forget all of this useless terminology and embrace yourself in your entirety, with no divisions.

Each time you indulge your physical senses, you are anchoring your consciousness to the physical dream; every smell, taste, sight, sound, or touch focuses more energy in the physical. Why do you think that ancient dreaming portals like the pyramids or catacombs were designed to eliminate the engagement of the senses? They purposefully removed light, sound, smell, and taste, and allowed the dreamers to loosen their connection to their physical bodies and heighten their focus on their light bodies.

Dissociation

As a small boy, my parents frequently used to take me to the mall. The crowds and the noise overwhelmed me practically every time. But it wasn't only the noise that bothered me; it was also the "psychic" or mental noise of all the people. I felt like I was being bombarded by sensory input.

Within ten minutes, my physical body would become very hot and my arms and legs would start to feel thick, heavy, and fat. Then my body would suddenly get thinner and very far away. My ears would buzz and ring and then be filled with a rushing sound just before they plugged up. Colors would swirl and I would feel sick to my stomach.

Then the being that I knew as "me" would come up out of the top of my head, bringing a sense of relief, but also making me feel very far away and disconnected, like I was back in my bed dreaming the whole nightmare. I had trouble making my arms and legs move, and when I talked, it felt like a stranger with a heavy voice was speaking through me, saying things that I would never dream of saying around my parents.

My somberness and withdrawal were always apparent, and I usually ran into people or things because it was difficult to control this machine called a "body." I had split perception, too, seeing people and the mall from just above my head and vaguely from somewhere above the crowds. I was clammy and feverish.

Within a few hours of returning to the safety of home, my second chakra would begin to glow again, arousing me and causing me to feel very vulnerable and exposed. Then my body would be flooded with the most intense and wonderful thickness, a rush of sexuality, fire, joy, and deep emotion as my light body reconnected with my physical body.

In my mid-twenties, I found out that this was a clinical condition known as dissociation, or being "split off" from reality, and that many war veterans experience it. But it was almost another ten years before I understood that these were actually out-of-body experiences that occurred while I was awake.

Out-of-Body Experiences

Many are familiar with out-of-body experiences from stories of people who suddenly wake up in the middle of the night or during surgery to see their physical body asleep in bed or on the operating table. People who have found themselves in life-threatening situations often say that an angel or other being assisted them.

There are stories of children who disappear for hours and don't even realize that they've been gone. Others experience missing time or have a near-death experience. These are all out-of-body experiences, or interactions with your light body. You have out-of-body experiences every night, whether you remember them or not.

Your light body can be activated in life-threatening situations; it simply takes over. Fear, anesthesia, and sleep all produce a lapse in your rationality and perception. Once there is a gap in your otherwise seamless mental chatter and energetic programming, your light body has the opportunity to do its thing.

When you are conscious and your light body takes over, you will feel like you're dreaming or like things are in slow motion. You may experience a very strong déjà vu, or feel like you were somewhere else witnessing the situation.

Sleepwalking occurs when your light body is out and your brain is worried or stressed about something from your daily life; your brain attempts to unwind the stress by walking your physical body through it. Light bodies communicate with each other constantly, planning and arranging "chance" meetings or other events.

None of this is to say that angels or other energetic entities do not exist. We just don't have a clue as to the abilities or manifestations of our own light bodies.

Children and Out-of-Body Experiences

If you have children or are around them much, take some time to ask them about their own experiences. You will be thoroughly shocked. Children have complete other worlds that they are involved in but rarely talk about. These worlds are eventually forgotten as they grow into adulthood. Because these worlds have no link to "reality," they are shifted back into the subconscious where they only appear in dreams.

Give children a diary or tape recorder and encourage them to keep a record of their experiences. You will have given them an invaluable gift. They will either maintain a conscious link to other worlds as they grow older, or at least have a key to reopen those worlds in adulthood.

Children in overwhelming situations often exhibit "antisocial" behavior—nervousness, fidgeting, hypersensitivity, withdrawal, crying, anger, or acting up. This is a surefire signal that they are out of their bodies. This freaks out other kids and causes hysteria and panic. Since the adults in charge of these children have forgotten about their own light bodies, they try to discipline the child. Some even go so far as to label them with moronic terms like ADHD. And then to compound the problem, they desensitize and immobilize them with prescription drugs.

Prescription drugs overheat the liver and kidneys, inciting even more fear in the already confused child and pushing their light body further away. The child has *no* idea what's going on, and will either behave as if stuck in a nightmare or as if he or she is dying. A child in this state *demands* your utmost care—reassurance, rest, superior food (not hot dogs or soda), peace and quiet, or a chance to run freely outdoors to help dissipate the fear. The child needs your groundedness and the removal of the shitty psychological labels and their accompanying stigmas. Get rid of the goddamn drugs.

Reconnecting with children and treating them as adults in little bodies will give you a glimpse of your own forgotten worlds. The children will give you many gifts. If a child is in an out-of-body state, remember that there is nothing abnormal about it. The light body functions in and out of the physical body. Both states are productive, and both should be developed and understood.

When your light body is within your physical body, you are in love—and lust—with everything and everyone. Your senses burst with a richness you haven't had since you were a child. The Earth becomes alive, and all violence and frustration vanish.

When your light body is outside your physical body, it instantly registers energetic impressions from other people and other worlds—"psychic" and intuitive information. It sees the illusory or dreamlike nature of the physical world and the ego, and it instantly recognizes Truth. It can also create stress and agitation if the process of separation is not understood.

Assist any children you come into contact with in grounding themselves and making their physical bodies into secure and healthy homes for their light bodies. *Show them* through your example the depths that are attainable when the brain is quiet, unhurried, and open. The more you're in your own body, the more you will be able to communicate and relate to the children. Give them the ability to navigate in all worlds.

Merging the Two Worlds

Enlightenment is a full state of consciousness, *without any unconscious or subconscious*. It is pure, one hundred percent awareness—asleep or awake.

Our physical and light bodies are supposed to work together as partners, but they have been alienated from each other. The only time they still have any success in communicating with each other is in our dreams. So often we wake up, remembering only bits and pieces, but having this feeling in our bones that we're missing the best parts of our dreams *and* our lives. The light body and the physical body need to merge, to meld into one solid unit—never splintered, never differentiated, never apart. Then your dreams become conscious. And when you're awake, you are able to see beyond the veil that separates the worlds.

This is why it is crucial to love both your physical body and your light body. It is imperative that you care for both. It is tantamount that you understand and embrace both. Balance your north pole and your south pole. Turn off your rational thoughts and turn on your feelings. Activate and never repress your chakra emotions. Eat perfect food, sleep perfectly, play and exercise perfectly, and keep your body light and unencumbered. Only a fresh mind can hear the messages of your light body. Only a mind that is not disturbed by harsh frequencies, chatter, and indulgence can feel the subtle vibrations of your light body. Only a light mind that has released its burdens is *quick enough* to register the fleeting impressions from other worlds.

We are living in a physical world. So intuiting an energetic Truth is only half the battle. Making that Truth *live* in the physical world is its fulfillment.

The light body is power and potentiality. Merge and *return to your godhood*. This is no woo-woo New Age bullshit. This is the fantasy activated into reality. Being "raised from the dead" or "reborn" is a reference to the light body being "born" absolutely into the physical body. Your mind can understand this later, after your body understands it first.

The world of the light body is the ultimate frontier—the ultimate adventure—and it is through the tangible and conscious witnessing of the world of the light body *within* the world of the physical body that we can catch a glimpse of the full-blown totality of ourselves.

Now you realize that the physical world is also a dream. This is the presence of your light body's awareness within and through your physical body. It results in a very distinct feeling of standing outside the force of time. Normally, you are only aware of your existence through the mirror of self-reflection, or through the memory of an event immediately *after* its occurrence. The presence of your light body's awareness within your daily consciousness, however, enables you to become aware of your own existence *as you create it*. A déjà vu is one result of this merging.

Other worlds will not even exist in your paradigm until you have attained a similarly connected and elevated energetic state. You won't even have a clue about their existence. This is a built-in safeguard, preventing people who have not done their homework from causing mischief in worlds that have evolved beyond ours. To someone in a disconnected state, it's only a fairy tale.

Conscious Dreaming and Frequency Matching

Have you ever felt like you're just about to remember something major, maybe even something not of this world, but couldn't quite get it? Have you ever wondered why you've never been thoroughly happy or completely satisfied? Have you ever longed for something or someone and wondered whether or not you made them up? Have you ever had a dream that was so real that you wish it had been? Have you ever seen a random stranger on the street and suddenly had a feeling that you've spoken with them recently? Do you have any memories that don't seem to fit in linearly with your life? Do you sometimes feel that some time is missing from your life, or that more time was inserted? Do you feel like your true friends and family are not here? Do you feel like science hasn't really proven anything you didn't already know?

One evening I was listening to a collection of songs. Then I went to bed. The next morning, I woke up and started thinking about some things that I needed to take care of. I noticed that one of the faster, more motivating songs was playing in the background in my head. About ten minutes later, I started to fall back asleep. My body and mind relaxed and let go, and the fast song immediately switched to a different and more emotional slow song. Then I remembered the rest of my early morning dream.

Too often, people wake up and remember only bits and pieces of their dreams. Or they can't remember any dreams, so they think they don't dream. But nothing could be further from the truth. People don't remember dreams because the moment they wake up their brains switch into high gear, processing, thinking, talking, debating, or worrying over yesterday's events or today's "what-ifs?" Their brains shift from cycling at the lower frequencies where dreams occur to the frazzled frequencies of thought and stress.

Deep dreams are filled with moods, colors, sensations, and emotions. This is the world of feeling, the world of your chakra energy and your light body. To remember your dreams when you wake up, you must maintain or at least match the frequencies you were in during your dreams. If you remember only bits and pieces, then you still have not gone low enough.

Your mind must be empty and still. Your body must be relaxed and unworried. This is where recapitulation, meditation, physical health, proper diet and exercise, freedom from diseases of the mind, peace in your relationships, the proper utilization of sexual energy, monatomic elements, balanced poles, and power coupled with joy all finally culminate. You are learning to align your body and mind with different frequencies.

The lower you go in your frequency matching, the closer you get to the world of your light body and total consciousness. If you want to remember your lost memories, then you must shift your frequency back to that time and *mood*. If you want to perceive the totality of your existence in all worlds and perceive other energies, then you have to open up all your frequencies, simultaneously. Conscious dreaming is only *one* aspect of total consciousness.

The Process

In our society, sleep is "normally" an *unconscious* state. Many people prefer it and desire to be comatose because any residual consciousness would register the nightmares that they are plagued with and trying to avoid.

When your mind and body are exhausted from the day, they lose consciousness in order to rest and repair themselves. Conscious dreaming has the potential to occur when your mind and body do not need to become unconscious at night.

Conscious dreaming cannot occur if you think too much. Thinking, which includes reading and talking, moves energy to the back of the brain. Your upper back, neck, and shoulders get really tight. You grind your teeth in your sleep and get cricks in your neck.

Conscious dreaming involves the front part of the brain, your third eye. When your mind stays calm and is not over-used during the day, you can recapitulate, lie down, and feel the energy move naturally to the front of your brain. You can watch yourself fall asleep while maintaining your conscious-ness. Your light body becomes aware of itself. You will feel more alive here than you've ever felt in your waking life.

If you engage your rational processes all day long, your brain is mush when you get home. Now it needs most of the night just to repair itself. Sometime in the morning, you start to have really vivid dreams, usually at the exact time you have to get up for work.

It takes a little over three years for your body to forget about sex. Your body carries the emotional memory that binds your second chakra energy to your sexuality instead of allowing it to be *available* for conscious dreaming. Don't encourage your mind to associate the sexual feeling with another person; keep it focused on yourself.

Passing out in the dream is conscious dreaming. This "passing out" *is* the ringing or rushing sound in the ears as your light body moves out. Then you will hear your physical body sighing, or "sah"-ing as it releases your light body. In the Egyptian Pyramid Texts, the word "sah" is used to actualize hidden powers.

Fall in lust with your nightly adventures. Desire sleep like you desire a woman. Know that no person can make you feel this way. You can't wait until you are alone with yourself. Your own body turns you on, and you freefall into that feeling and then release it within yourself. This is how you utilize sexual energy to ignite all your chakras. Strong emotion is what takes you there.

Time

Time is the movement of your consciousness as it desires to see what happens if it does this or makes that choice. When you are outside time, you wonder where you are and how you even got to this place. It's the biggest thrill, utterly expansive. All you can do is laugh and shake your head. You are timeless. There is no other place you desire to be.

You can disengage yourself from time by removing all things from your life that remind you of, or tie you to, time. Memories of events, conversations, thought, sensory stimulations—anything that keeps your consciousness focused on the progression of time and events.

Pyramids and other dreaming chambers shut out all sensory input. It's hard to imagine how unnerving this really is. Even if you think back on the darkest place you've ever been, eventually your eyes adjusted and you could see *something*.

But these dreaming chambers removed *all* light, outside sound, smell, taste, and human contact, thereby shutting down those parts of the brain and physical body. After a few days of this, different mechanisms in the body became active.

Upon emerging, the dreamers' heightened sensitivity to their light bodies and five senses would allow them to detect even the slightest energetic vibrations of others.

Who's Watching You?

I really enjoy watching ants. They're like little doggies rummaging around, sniffing out food. I have often wondered why they don't realize that we are looking at them. And that makes me wonder who's looking down at me.

Imagine if one ant suddenly looked up and started talking to you. Somehow, in the midst of his busy ant life and against all the odds of being an ant, he had stored enough energy to become conscious of your presence and was trying to talk to you. This is how it is between humans and the Source, or between us and energies of greater consciousness.

Against the odds of being human, and amidst our day-to-day chatter and rushing around, we somehow store enough energy to become aware of, and communicate with, other forms of awareness. And suddenly, one of them realizes that one of the *billions* of humans is attempting to communicate with them. And they pay attention, because they are curious, too. They are already here with us. All we need is more energy.

Seeing Other Worlds

Your consciousness flashes in and out of other realities on a moment-to-moment basis. The reality that you find yourself in is a choice. This, now, is your primary reality, but it doesn't have to be. Your ultimate power is to be aware of all of your realities at all times.

Seeing other worlds is a lot easier than you might think. Holding the view of them can be difficult, however. It's all about not flinching and missing the moment.

The first time I saw another reality, I thought it was a meaningless daydream. I was staring out my bedroom window just before sunset, watching the eucalyptus trees blowing in a mild Santa Ana wind. I allowed myself to follow the silence as it led me into a trance and my brain shut off. I diverged my eyes and engaged my deep vision. A white light flashed, and then I saw faces superimposed on the branches and leaves of the trees.

As I relaxed my stomach and solar plexus, and resisted the urge to flinch and rationalize, the faces became clearer and my solar plexus warmed up. It felt thoroughly normal and practically boring, like I was watching a group of people mingling at a party. Yet it was very real. I felt like I had walked in on a gathering; some of them even *looked back at me,* and their glances had awareness.

The best time to experiment is just after sunset as the light becomes blue-black. Sit comfortably in the dark and stare out a window into the twilight. Allow your thoughts to ramble as they will without latching onto, feeding, or following any of them. Relax your body and breathe peacefully. Don't play any music or burn any incense or candles—limit all sensory input. It's too easy to get distracted. Let your eyes diverge and notice the hues surrounding the trees and plants, and some of the black shadows.

Reduce your blinking. Blinking interrupts the direct flow of energy into your brain and allows your brain a split second to reimpose its established interpretations of energy onto the actual energy flowing into your eyes. Squint or close your eyes halfway to moisten them.

By reducing the amount of blinking, the influx of energy now has a chance to maintain other colorations or patterns that you have been taught to eliminate or skew. You will pick up impressions of energy and parallel existences. This occurs just after the dark halo surrounds your vision.

As you do this, your eyes will start to play weird little tricks. At first, you'll sink into the blue-blackness and your body will feel as though it's being pleasantly submerged in the ocean of the night. The shadows will subside and your vision will become more clear. But at some point, there will be a flash of white light, as if someone turned on a lamp. But nobody did. Immediately after the flash, you will get a fleeting image of some otherness and then feel it pulling you in. Let go.

You may have to work at this regularly to try to overcome your fear and resist jerking yourself back. The mind is very protective of its beliefs about your sanity, and you will probably run away from it time and time again. It's as if the mind just cannot allow other worlds to exist for fear of losing itself. But it won't be lost.

When you perceive other energies or worlds, you use your system of symbols, words, or images to *interpret* that system as best you can. But it is not accurate; it is only approximate. You distort the energy of other worlds because you do not possess *their* system of symbols, and their systems are needed if you want to see their energetic creations or complexities in the same *manner* that they do. Their creations are different from our own. If you remove your system of symbols, you will perceive only energy and its intention. Otherwise you will probably see little green monsters and UFOs.

Multidimensionality

In the dead of night when all is still, when a wind chime softly plays one note once, then twice, you can be sure that it's not the wind.

You are a multidimensional being. You can be in more than one place at the same time. Others can participate, and you don't have to be asleep. It could be called an out-of-body experience or conscious dreaming, except that you're not asleep.

I've been getting ready for bed at night and seen the hovering presence of a woman I knew and had seen earlier that day. She was asleep. I was not. I knew she was dreaming, and that she came to say "hi" and see what I was really about.

I have been on the floor in the middle of a Pilates exercise when I noticed that my father was hovering over my kitchen. At first, it didn't even faze me—it was my father and he was in my kitchen. He had just been there a few days ago. I wasn't thinking about him or about anything at all. But he was physically having dinner in a restaurant two hundred miles away and had just cracked his tooth. We were both fully awake.

I have been sitting on the toilet while my girlfriend was three hundred miles away hanging out with some close friends. They were considering some things regarding me and asking my permission. When I spoke with my girlfriend later, I told her that it had been at 5:50 P.M. She affirmed the time.

I was dozing in and out in my recliner one evening when I noticed a man standing in front of me just to my left. My girlfriend was in her chair on my right. They were both within a few feet of me. When I awoke, I told my girlfriend that a very old and new friend had just been visiting. He was as solid as my girlfriend, and comforting to have nearby, but he did not exist in a physical form.

I knew a young girl who was from the same energetic family as a famous pop singer. The young girl lived on a farm with a religious family that raised chickens. She hardly bathed. The pop singer lived the glamorous wild life and traveled the world. It was a fascinating and perfect dichotomy. When I looked into the young girl's eyes, her light body told me she was exploring two sides of this dream simultaneously. Both of them winked at me.

I have been having sex with one woman while another, who knew where I was, sent her consciousness to observe the energetic exchange. I have been at work when a girlfriend's emotion came and wrapped her arms around me from behind. I felt her as if she were actually behind me, breathing on my neck. I have seen strangers in my early morning dreams that I met in person later that day. I also have a friend in southern California who likes to check in from time to time, but he's very careful not to interfere.

An old, sickly cat that I was caring for died. I put him in

a box in my trunk and started the drive to the vet to have the body taken care of. The cat's consciousness asked permission to look through my eyes as we drove on the bluffs over the ocean. I agreed, and felt him looking one last time at the beauty of the Earth. After I left the body, the cat left me. I was in a deep daze.

One morning, in the early light, I was putting on my pants to go to work when a close relative suddenly showed up in my bedroom. I knew he was having surgery that morning, but didn't know the exact time. I told him, as his light body told me simultaneously, that everything felt just fine. I showed him some energy work. I called later, and found out that he had arrived in my room within two minutes after the nurse had administered his anesthesia. I had only seen him out of his body a couple of times before in my lifetime, usually when he was asleep and troubled.

Many times I have felt afraid for people who were making long or vulnerable trips. Finally, I realized that it was *their* fear that I was picking up on, and that it was triggering my own long-lost fears. I had to learn to distinguish, and walk through my fears as well. As my friend Court says, "This is mine. This is not mine."

Once I and some others were helping to pack up some books for an elderly man who was moving out of his house. His wife had died recently and he was having trouble taking care of himself. I was exploring by myself down in his huge basement, soaking up the strange moods and listening to the old left-behind feelings while looking for a bathroom. I walked into a green, musty room and spotted a bathroom to my right. As I made for the bathroom, I noticed an elderly woman behind me to my left. She was standing *in* the middle of an old, stained mattress in the back corner of the room. I saw instantly that it was the man's deceased wife, hovering in and over the bed that she had died upon. I faced her squarely, watching myself drift between the two realities, and told her everything was taken care of and that she was free to go without fear. I raised my hands and felt a rush of energy go out to her. Her presence lingered for a time, but most of her energy moved on.

A singer I had an unusual affinity for died suddenly, and then decided to come and live with me for about two weeks. She followed me around the house and around town, watching and listening. She wanted to hear some of her own songs through my ears and feelings. She was afraid and not ready to go. She missed her family and friends, and felt like she had made a big mistake. A video about her accident aired on television and we watched it together, connecting with her loved ones. She finally realized that she had already made her choice, and that she had friends in other worlds. I walked with her to the other side, and set her safely on her way. Then she left. Just recently, I saw another woman from her energetic family at a bank and saw the singer's eyes as the new woman smiled at me with deep affection, waving like she knew me.

I have had presences in my dreams that are as conscious of me as I am of them. You can detect their presence because their eyes will sizzle or the object will hiss. Whose dream is this, anyway?

These are examples of multidimensionality in action. Both people don't have to be cognizant of the event. Actually, neither does. It happens all the time regardless of the awareness of either. But if you have enough space between your thoughts and you cultivate sensitivity, you will know when an aspect of someone is present and focused on you. You will know it as if they were suddenly standing next to you.

The Gift

Susan and I were sleeping in our separate beds in a hotel room in Burbank. I was on my back and she was on her side facing me. I faded in and out...

I come to in the passenger seat of a beat-up old pickup truck. Suddenly, a man with long dark hair and dark leathery skin appears out of nowhere and rapidly advances toward me, a small-caliber handgun gripped disturbingly in his filthy oversized hand. His eyes sizzle with anger and his teeth grate with malice as he lifts his rigid arm and points the gun straight at my face.

Crack! Crack! Crack! The bullets slam against the windshield. My bowels loosen. He lurches onto my side of the truck and grabs the windshield with the gun still in his hand, his looming face and sinister presence engulfing me in his darkness. Crack! The gun goes off again, the bullet grazing sideways across the windshield.

Dark heat and impotence consume me now, and I sink down into my seat, my limbs cold with horror. But quite unexpectedly, I remember a friend telling me about tribes that teach their children how to face their fears in their dreams. It registers instantaneously, and my body thickens and rises up above the window.

The strength amasses in my arms and they grow thick as tree trunks. My fingers turn into guns on both hands and I thrust them at him with their white-hot and blistering intent. He sinks helplessly down to the ground.

Now I am practically hysterical with rage, and my voice cracks as I scream and yell with an uncontrolled shrillness born of the adrenaline rush. He must give me a gift for having faced him down! So I demand one, still shaking. He pulls a thick permanent marker and a piece of white paper shaped like a snowflake out of his back pocket. He draws a power image on it, something with a cryptic tinge of mystery. And even though I can tell it's mental and not powerful in and of itself, I accept it and feel a jolt of power when I take it from his shriveling hand.

But then something deep inside of me lets go of my puny mental thoughts of power and image, and I slip into a temporary void—searching, waiting. The blackness gets deeper and wider, and a tinge of excitement grows beyond my belly. I sense something ominous approach. I know it is the real gift. I can hardly stand it.

Cracking brilliantly out of the blackness thunders a thick white ball that explodes before me and sucks me helplessly into its womb. I am consumed like a rag doll by the omnipotent power and then mercilessly injected with the most flabbergasting light I have ever experienced. My body balloons beyond its regular capacity; I am stretched and jam-packed from within.

Back in Burbank, my body suddenly heaves up off the bed and my arms fling out to the sides. I wake up instantaneously to hear my body moaning involuntarily and to see Susan looking at me with drowsy incomprehension as I mumble indefinable words and names. My body collapses back onto the bed, and I pass out into a long and peaceful slumber.

Postscript

The Truth is that you don't need to practice any of these exercises *if* you can get out of the way of the natural unfoldment of the Source within you. You can just relax, smile, and be filled with the joy and power of your light body. The unfoldment will be your meditation. Your light body will flower according to its own design in its own time and way. It is playful, it is mysterious, and it is a thick and heady rousing. It is potent! Your light body is the magic genie trapped in the bottle.

You will be drawn perfectly to all events that give you the opportunity to walk deeply into the wholeness of your emotions. You will naturally desire the foods and sources that replenish your monatomic deficiencies. You will enter and exit relationships with an open heart and with absolute love. You will be awake and receptive to your unconscious self, and your body will always be in perfect balance. Your fear will be seen for what it is and will simply fall away. Your chakra energies will be free to mingle and develop, and your light body will playfully lead you to your destiny. It *can* be this way—if you let it.

Why ask why? Just accept it and do it. If you feel it, do it. There's no need to rationalize anything. You either like it or you don't. Maybe you're just trying to avoid your feelings by thinking about everything. Maybe part of your problem is trying to explain things to death and understand them logically. Maybe there is no logic in the world of the light body.

Maybe in the multidimensional world of the light body, things don't add up for a long time—or at all. Maybe the ripple that you start here and now with your nonsensical action won't affect this reality or any other for years or lifetimes, long after the ripple has been forgotten. Maybe you will never directly encounter the result or reap the benefit, but many others will.

You won't feel it until you *refuse* to speak about it. Feeling is within the silence. We are afraid to trust ourselves. We have been raised to doubt those things that cannot be "proved" by our brains and abstract patterns. The brain and logic do not belong here. Our feelings do. Our inner knowledge is ancient and needs no confirmation.

All of this talking, reading, and writing is not living. You already know all of this. Our light bodies communicate every night. So just live. Go play badminton, fly a kite, make some salsa, take a perfect dump, and be aware of every nuance. It's all inside you. Don't ask anyone for proof because you've already got all the proof you need. Revert to a world of *impressions*—turn inside.

Now you can throw away all of your books, including this one . . .

Resources and Suggested Reading

Clark, Hulda Regehr. 1995. *The Cure for All Diseases.* San Diego, Calif.: Pro-Motion Publishing.

Doreal. 2002. *The Emerald Tablets of Thoth-the-Atlantean.* Sedalia, Colo.: Brotherhood of the White Temple.

Emerson, Willis George. 1908. *The Smoky God.* Chicago: Forbes & Company.

Fallon, Sally, with Mary G. Enig. 2001. *Nourishing Traditions,* rev. 2nd ed. Washington, D.C.: New Trends Publishing.

Gardner, Laurence. 1999. *Genesis of the Grail Kings.* New York: Bantam Press.

———. 2003. *Lost Secrets of the Sacred Ark.* Hammersmith, London: Element (an imprint of HarperCollins).

Hudson, David. 1995. Lecture in Dallas, Texas. Transcribed from videotapes recorded by the Eclectic Viewpoint.

Lloyd, John Uri. 1896. *Etidorhpa.* Cincinnati, Ohio: The Robert Clarke Company.

Marciniak, Barbara. 1992. *Bringers of the Dawn.* Santa Fe, N.M.: Bear & Company.

McCabe, Ed. 2003. *Flood Your Body with Oxygen,* 6th ed. Miami Shores, Fla.: Energy Publications.

N. E. Thing Enterprises. 1995. *Magic Eye Gallery.* Kansas City, Mo.: Andrews and McMeel.

Roberts, Jane. 1994. *Seth Speaks.* San Rafael, Calif.: New World Library.

Schmid, Ron. 2003. *The Untold Story of Milk.* Winona Lake, Ind.: New Trends Publishing.

Steinman, David, and R. Michael Wisner. 1996. *Living Healthy in a Toxic World.* New York: Berkeley Publishing Group.

Becoming a Man of Power

Vonderplanitz, Aajonus. 2005. *Primal Diet: We Want to Live.* Los Angeles: Carnelian Bay/Castle Press.

lewfh.tripod.com/thehealingpropertiesofwater—The healing properties of chi in structured water.

www.aloelife.com—Aloe products.

www.aquasunozone.com—Ozonators and ionizers.

www.asc-alchemy.com—Monatomic elements, molecularly restructured water, and a wealth of great information.

www.celtic-seasalt.com—Celtic Sea Salt, fermented vegetables.

www.classicalpilates.net—Classical Pilates DVDs.

www.drclarkstore.com—Dr. Clark products and cleansing kits.

www.gemcultures.com—Dairy cultures for raw milk.

www.h2o2oxytech.com—Food grade hydrogen peroxide.

www.Paulgrilleyyoga.com—Paul Grilley's Yin Yoga website.

www.ottlite.com—Ott-Lite True Color full spectrum light bulbs.

www.ourhollowearth.com—Inner Earth resources and expeditions.

www.pyramidtexts.com—Original translations of the pyramid texts.

www.rejuvenative.com—Fermented vegetables, fresh raw nut and seed butters.

www.tomorrowsworld.com—Organic clothes, bedding and clean products.

Matt Guest lives in California.
Please visit
www.The LightBody.com
for further info and
links to weekly Internet broadcasts.

HAMPTON ROADS
PUBLISHING COMPANY, INC.

Thank you for reading *Becoming a Man of Power.* Hampton Roads is proud to publish an extensive array of books on the topics discussed in this book, topics such as cultivating awareness, Toltec beliefs, lucid dreaming, and more. Please take a look at the following selection or visit us anytime on the web: www.hrpub.com.

Dreaming While Awake
Techniques for 24-Hour Lucid Dreaming
Arnold Mindell, Ph.D.

According to groundbreaking psychotherapist Mindell, we all dream all day long whether we know it or not. Mindell shows us why to tap into this constant stream of messages from the dreamworld—"flirts" as he calls them—and how 24-hour lucid dreaming can serve as preventive medicine for both health and personal relationships.

ISBN 1-57174-359-6 · $15.95
Paperback · 272 pages

Traveling with Power
The Exploration and Development of Perception
Ken Eagle Feather

Beginning with his apprenticeship to nagual shaman don Juan Matus, Eagle Feather takes readers on a trip along the many winding paths of perception. You'll learn how to explore various modes of expanded consciousness using shamanism, lucid dreaming, out-of-body experiences, and more.

ISBN 1-878901-28-1 · $12.95
Paperback · 280 pages

www.hrpub.com   1-800-766-8009

Tracking Freedom
A Guide for Personal Evolution
Ken Eagle Feather

Building upon the teachings of Toltec seer don Juan Matus, Tracking Freedom shows you how to read auras and other energy fields, balance chakra energies for personal growth, and find and travel a path with heart.

ISBN 1-57174-093-7 · $13.95
Paperback · 280 pages

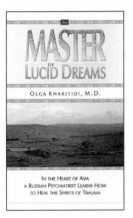

The Master of Lucid Dreams
Olga Kharitidi, M.D.,
author of *Entering the Circle*

At the invitation of an ancient secret brotherhood, psychiatrist Kharitidi travels to exotic Samarkand in the heart of Asia to undergo a profound shamanic healing. Her story reveals a different path to true healing that is available to us all.

ISBN 1-57174-329-4 · $14.95
Paperback · 240 pages

The Road to Power
Taking Control of Your Life
Barbara Berger

The same tools Berger used to master her life can be found in The Road to Power. Berger offers nearly effortless yet effective suggestions for creating, unleashing, and maintaining your full power and potential. Included are techniques for learning the power of saying "no," letting go of negativity, the hidden benefits of secrecy, and much more.

ISBN 1-57174-443-6 · $14.95
Paperback · 208 pages

www.hrpub.com   1-800-766-8009

Hampton Roads Publishing Company
. . . for the evolving human spirit

HAMPTON ROADS PUBLISHING COMPANY publishes
books on a variety of subjects, including metaphysics,
spirituality, health, visionary fiction, and other related
topics.

For a copy of our latest trade catalog, call toll-free,
800-766-8009, or send your name and address to:

HAMPTON ROADS PUBLISHING COMPANY, INC.
1125 STONEY RIDGE ROAD • CHARLOTTESVILLE, VA 22902
e-mail: hrpc@hrpub.com • Internet: www.hrpub.com